CIVILIZATION
AND ITS DISCONTENTS

SIGMUND FREUD, M.D., LL.D.

AUTHORIZED TRANSLATION

BY

JOAN RIVIERE

NEW YORK

JONATHAN CAPE & HARRISON SMITH

PRINTED IN THE UNITED STATES
BY THE DE VINNE-HALLENBECK COMPANY
AND BOUND BY THE J. F. TAPLEY COMPANY

TRANSLATOR'S NOTE

My grateful thanks are due to Fräulein Anna Freud, Dr. Ernest Jones and Mr. James Strachey for their careful revision of the MS. of this translation and the many improvements they made in it, and also to Miss Ethel Colburn Mayne for her translations of the verse quoted.

J. R.

I

THE impression forces itself upon one that men measure by false standards, that everyone seeks power, success, riches for himself and admires others who attain them, while undervaluing the truly precious things in life. And yet, in making any general judgement of this kind one is in danger of forgetting the manifold variety of humanity and its mental life. There are certain men from whom their contemporaries do not withhold veneration, although their greatness rests on attributes and achievements which are completely foreign to the aims and ideals of the multitude. One might well be inclined to suppose that after all it is only a minority who appreciate these great men, while the majority cares nothing for them. But the discrepancy between men's opinions and their behaviour is so wide and their desires so many-sided that things are probably not so simple.

One of these exceptional men calls himself my friend in his letters to me. I had sent him my little book which treats of religion as an illusion and he answered that he agreed entirely with my views on religion, but that he was sorry I had not properly appreciated the ultimate source of religious sentiments. This consists in a peculiar feeling, which never leaves him personally, which he finds shared by many others, and which he may suppose millions more also experience. It is a feeling which he would like to call a sensation of ' eternity ', a feeling as of something limitless, unbounded, something ' oceanic '. It is, he says, a purely subjective experience, not an article of belief ; it implies no assurance of personal immortality, but it is the source of the religious spirit and is taken hold of by the various Churches and religious systems, directed by them into definite channels and also, no doubt, used up in them. One may rightly call oneself religious on the ground of this oceanic feeling alone, even though one reject all beliefs and all illusions.

These views, expressed by my friend whom I so greatly honour and who himself once in poetry described the magic of illusion, put me in a difficult position. I cannot discover this ' oceanic ' feeling in myself. It is not easy to deal scientifically with feelings. One may attempt to describe their physiological signs. Where that is impossible—I am afraid the oceanic feeling, too, will defy this kind of classification—nothing remains but to turn to the ideational content which most readily associates itself with the feeling. If I have understood my friend aright, he means the same thing as that consolation offered by an original and somewhat unconventional writer to his hero, contemplating suicide: 'Out of this world we cannot fall '.[1] So it is a feeling of indissoluble connection, of belonging inseparably to the external world as a whole. To me, personally, I may remark, this seems something more in the nature of an intellectual judgement, not, it is true, without any accompanying feeling-tone, but with one of a kind which characterizes other equally far-reaching reflections as well. I could not in my own person convince myself of the primary nature of such a feeling. But I cannot on that account deny that it in fact occurs in other people. One can only wonder whether it has been correctly interpreted and whether it is entitled to be acknowledged as the *fons et origo* of the whole need for religion.

I have nothing to suggest which could effectively settle the solution of this problem. The idea

---

[1] Christian Grabbe, *Hannibal* : Ja, aus der Welt werden wir nicht fallen. Wir sind einmal darin.'

that man should receive intimation of his connection with the surrounding world by a direct feeling which aims from the outset at serving this purpose sounds so strange and is so incongruous with the structure of our psychology that one is justified in attempting a psycho-analytic, that is, genetic explanation of such a feeling. Whereupon the following lines of thought present themselves. Normally there is nothing we are more certain of than the feeling of our self, our own ego. It seems to us an independent unitary thing, sharply outlined against everything else. That this is a deceptive appearance, and that on the contrary the ego extends inwards without any sharp delimitation, into an unconscious mental entity which we call the id and to which it forms a façade, was first discovered by psycho-analytic research, and the latter still has much to tell us about the relations of the ego to the id. But towards the outer world at any rate the ego seems to keep itself clearly and sharply outlined and delimited. There is only one state of mind in which it fails to do this—an unusual state, it is true, but not one that can be judged as pathological. At its height the state of being in love threatens to obliterate the boundaries between ego and object. Against all the evidence of his senses the man in love declares that he and his beloved are one, and is prepared to behave as if it were a fact. A thing that can be temporarily effaced by a physiological function must also of course be liable to disturbance by morbid processes. From pathology we have come to know a large number of states in which the boundary lines between ego and outer world become uncertain, or in which they are actually incorrectly perceived—cases in which parts of a man's own body, even component parts of his own mind, perceptions, thoughts, feelings, appear to him alien and not belonging to himself; other cases in which a man ascribes to the external world things that clearly originate in himself, and that ought to be acknowledged by him. So the ego's cognizance of itself is subject to disturbance, and the boundaries between it and the outer world are not immovable.

Further reflection shows that the adult's sense of his own ego cannot have been the same from the beginning. It must have undergone a development, which naturally cannot be demonstrated, but which admits of reconstruction with a fair degree of probability.[1] When the infant at the breast receives stimuli, he cannot as yet distinguish

[1] Cf. the considerable volume of work on this topic dating from that of Ferenczi ('Stages in the Development of the Sense of Reality', 1913) up to Federn's contributions, 1926, 1927 and later.

whether they come from his ego or from the outer
world. He learns it gradually as the result of
various exigencies. It must make the strongest
impression on him that many sources of excita
tion, which later on he will recognize as his own
bodily organs, can provide him at any time with
sensations, whereas others become temporarily out
of his reach—amongst these what he wants most
of all, his mother's breast—and reappear only as
a result of his cries for help. Thus an 'object'
first presents itself to the ego as something existing
'outside', which is only induced to appear by a
particular act. A further stimulus to the growth
and formation of the ego, so that it becomes something more than a bundle of sensations, *i.e.* recognizes an 'outside', the external world, is afforded
by the frequent, unavoidable and manifold pains
and unpleasant sensations which the pleasure-
principle, still in unrestricted domination, bids it
abolish or avoid. The tendency arises to dissociate
from the ego everything which can give rise to
pain, to cast it out and create a pure pleasure-ego,
in contrast to a threatening 'outside', not-self.
The limits of this primitive pleasure-ego cannot
escape readjustment through experience. Much
that the individual wants to retain because it is
pleasure-giving is nevertheless part not of the ego

but of an object; and much that he wishes to eject because it torments him yet proves to be inseparable from the ego, arising from an inner source. He learns a method by which, through deliberate use of the sensory organs and suitable muscular movements, he can distinguish between internal and external—what is part of the ego and what originates in the outer world—and thus he makes the first step towards the introduction of the reality-principle which is to control his development further. This capacity for distinguishing which he learns of course serves a practical purpose, that of enabling him to defend himself against painful sensations felt by him or threatening him. Against certain painful excitations from within the ego has only the same means of defence as that employed against pain coming from without, and this is the starting-point of important morbid disturbances.

In this way the ego detaches itself from the external world. It is more correct to say: Originally the ego includes everything, later it detaches from itself the external world. The ego-feeling we are aware of now is thus only a shrunken vestige of a far more extensive feeling—a feeling which embraced the universe and expressed an inseparable connection of the ego with the external world. If we may suppose that this primary ego-feeling has been preserved in the minds of many people—to a greater or lesser extent—it would co-exist like a sort of counterpart with the narrower and more sharply outlined ego-feeling of maturity, and the ideational content belonging to it would be precisely the notion of limitless extension and oneness with the universe—the same feeling as that described by my friend as ' oceanic '. But have we any right to assume that the original type of feeling survives alongside the later one which has developed from it?

Undoubtedly we have : there is nothing unusual in such a phenomenon, whether in the psychological or in other spheres. Where animals are concerned we hold the view that the most highly developed have arisen from the lowest. Yet we still find all the simple forms alive to-day. The great saurians are extinct and have made way for the mammals, but a typical representative of them, the crocodile, is still living among us. The analogy may be too remote, and it is also weakened by the fact that the surviving lower species are not as a rule the true ancestors of the present-day more highly developed types. The intermediate members have mostly died out and are known to us only through reconstruction. In the realm of mind, on the other hand, the primitive type is so commonly preserved alongside the transformations which have developed out of it that it is superfluous to give instances in proof of it. When this happens, it is usually the result of a bifurcation in development. One quantitative part of an attitude or an impulse has survived unchanged while another has undergone further development.

This brings us very close to the more general problem of conservation in the mind, which has so far hardly been discussed, but is so interesting and important that we may take the opportunity to pay it some attention, even though its relevance is not immediate. Since the time when we recognized the error of supposing that ordinary forgetting signified destruction or annihilation of the memory-trace, we have been inclined to the opposite view that nothing once formed in the mind could ever perish, that everything survives in some way or other, and is capable under certain conditions of being brought to light again, as, for instance, when regression extends back far enough. One might try to picture to oneself what this assumption signifies by a comparison taken from another field. Let us choose the history of the Eternal City as an example.[1] Historians tell us that the oldest Rome

[1] According to *The Cambridge Ancient History*, vol. vii., 1928, ' The Founding of Rome ', by Hugh Last.

of all was the *Roma quadrata*, a fenced settlement
on the Palatine.   Then followed the phase of the
Septimontium, when the colonies on the different
hills united together; then the town which was
bounded by the Servian wall; and later still,
after all the transformations in the periods of the
republic and the early Caesars, the city which
the Emperor Aurelian enclosed by his walls.   We
will not follow the changes the city went through
any further, but will ask ourselves what traces
of these early stages in its history a visitor to
Rome may still find to-day, if he goes equipped
with the most complete historical and topographical knowledge.   Except for a few gaps,
he will see the wall of Aurelian almost unchanged.   He can find sections of the Servian
rampart at certain points where it has been
excavated and brought to light.   If he knows
enough—more than present-day archaeology—he
may perhaps trace out in the structure of the town
the whole course of this wall and the outline of
Roma quadrata.   Of the buildings which once
occupied this ancient ground-plan he will find
nothing, or but meagre fragments, for they exist no
longer.   With the best information about Rome of
the republican era, the utmost he could achieve
would be to indicate the sites where the temples

and public buildings of that period stood. These places are now occupied by ruins, but the ruins are not those of the early buildings themselves but of restorations of them in later times after fires and demolitions. It is hardly necessary to mention that all these remains of ancient Rome are found woven into the fabric of a great metropolis which has arisen in the last few centuries since the Renaissance. There is assuredly much that is ancient still buried in the soil or under the modern buildings of the town. This is the way in which we find antiquities surviving in historic cities like Rome.

Now let us make the fantastic supposition that Rome were not a human dwelling-place, but a mental entity with just as long and varied a past history : that is, in which nothing once constructed had perished, and all the earlier stages of development had survived alongside the latest. This would mean that in Rome the palaces of the Caesars were still standing on the Palatine and the Septizonium of Septimius Severus was still tower-ing to its old height ; that the beautiful statues were still standing in the colonnade of the Castle of St. Angelo, as they were up to its siege by the Goths, and so on. But more still: where the Palazzo Caffarelli stands there would also be, without this

B

being removed, the Temple of Jupiter Capitolinus, not merely in its latest form, moreover, as the Romans of the Caesars saw it, but also in its earliest shape, when it still wore an Etruscan design and was adorned with terra-cotta antifixae.   Where the Coliseum stands now we could at the same time admire Nero's Golden House ; on the Piazza of the Pantheon we should find not only the Pantheon of to-day as bequeathed to us by Hadrian, but on the same site also Agrippa's original edifice ; indeed, the same ground would support the church of Santa Maria sopra Minerva and the old temple over which it was built.   And the observer would need merely to shift the focus of his eyes, perhaps, or change his position, in order to call up a view of either the one or the other.

There is clearly no object in spinning this fantasy further ; it leads to the inconceivable, or even to absurdities.   If we try to represent his-torical sequence in spatial terms, it can only be done by juxtaposition in space ; the same space will not hold two contents.   Our attempt seems like an idle game ; it has only one justification : it shows us how far away from mastering the idiosyn-crasies of mental life we are by treating them in terms of visual representation.

There is one objection, though, to which we must

pay attention.   It questions our choosing in particular the past history of a *city* to liken to the past
of the mind.   Even for mental life our assumption
that everything past is preserved holds good only
on condition that the organ of the mind remains
intact and its structure has not been injured by
traumas or inflammation.   Destructive influences
comparable to these morbid agencies are never
lacking in the history of any town, even if it has
had a less chequered past than Rome, even if, like
London, it has hardly ever been pillaged by an
enemy.   Demolitions and the erection of new
buildings in the place of old occur in cities which
have had the most peaceful existence ;   therefore a
town is from the outset unsuited for the comparison
I have made of it with a mental organism.

We admit this objection ;   we will abandon our
search for a striking effect of contrast and turn
to what is after all a closer object of comparison,
the body of an animal or human being.   But here,
too, we find the same thing.   The early stages of
development are in no sense still extant ; they have
been absorbed into the later features for which they
supplied the material.   The embryo cannot be
demonstrated in the adult ;   the thymus gland of
childhood is replaced after puberty by connective
tissue but no longer exists itself ;   in the marrow-

bone of a grown man I can, it is true, trace the outline of the childish bone-structure, but this latter
no longer survives in itself—it lengthened and
thickened until it reached its final form.   The fact is
that a survival of all the early stages alongside the
final form is only possible in the mind, and that it
is impossible for us to represent a phenomenon of
this kind in visual terms.

Perhaps we are going too far with this conclusion.   Perhaps we ought to be content with the
assertion that what is past in the mind *can* survive
and need not necessarily perish.   It is always
possible that even in the mind much that is old
may be so far obliterated or absorbed—whether
normally or by way of exception—that it cannot
be restored or reanimated by any means, of that
survival of it is always connected with certain
favourable conditions.   It is possible, but we know
nothing about it.   We can only be sure that it is
more the rule than the exception for the past to
survive in the mind.

Thus we are entirely willing to acknowledge
that the ' oceanic ' feeling exists in many people,
and we are disposed to relate it to an early stage
in ego-feeling ;   the further question then arises
what claim this feeling has to be regarded as the
source of the need for religion.

To me this claim does not seem very forcible. Surely a feeling can only be a source of energy when it is itself the expression of a strong need. The derivation of a need for religion from the child's feeling of helplessness and the longing it evokes for a father seems to me incontrovertible, especially since this feeling is not simply carried on from childhood days but is kept alive perpetually by the fear of what the superior power of fate will bring. I could not point to any need in childhood so strong as that for a father's protection. Thus the part played by the ' oceanic ' feeling, which I suppose seeks to reinstate limitless narcissism, cannot possibly take the first place. The derivation of the religious attitude can be followed back in clear outline as far as the child's feeling of helplessness. There may be something else behind this, but for the present it is wrapped in obscurity.

I can imagine that the oceanic feeling could become connected with religion later on. That feeling of oneness with the universe which is its ideational content sounds very like a first attempt at the consolations of religion, like another way taken by the ego of denying the dangers it sees threatening it in the external world. I must again confess that I find it very difficult to work with these intangible quantities. Another friend of mine, whose insatiable scientific curiosity has impelled him to the most out-of-the-way researches and to the acquisition of encyclopaedic knowledge, has assured me that the Yogi by their practices of withdrawal from the world, concentrating attention on bodily functions, peculiar methods of breathing, actually are able to produce new sensations and diffused feelings in themselves which he regards as regressions to primordial, deeply buried mental states. He sees in them a physiological foundation, so to speak, of much of the wisdom of mysticism. There would be connections to be made here with many obscure modifications of mental life, such as trance and ecstasy. But I am moved to exclaim, in the words of Schiller's diver :

Who breathes overhead in the rose-tinted light may be glad !

II

IN my *Future of an Illusion*[1] I was concerned
much less with the deepest sources of religious
feeling than with what the ordinary man
understands by his religion, that system of doc-
trines and pledges that on the one hand explains
the riddle of this world to him with an enviable
completeness, and on the other assures him that a
solicitous Providence is watching over him and
will make up to him in a future existence for any
shortcomings in this life. The ordinary man cannot imagine this Providence in any other form but
that of a greatly exalted father, for only such a
one could understand the needs of the sons of
men, or be softened by their prayers and placated
by the signs of their remorse. The whole thing is
so patently infantile, so incongruous with reality,
that to one whose attitude to humanity is friendly
it is painful to think that the great majority of
mortals will never be able to rise above this view
of life. It is even more humiliating to discover

[1] 1927. London: Hogarth Press, 1928.

what a large number of those alive to-day, who must see that this religion is not tenable, yet try to defend it inch by inch, as if with a series of pitiable rearguard actions. One would like to count oneself among the believers, so as to admonish the philosophers who try to preserve the God of religion by substituting for him an impersonal, shadowy, abstract principle, and say, ' Thou shalt not take the name of the Lord thy God in vain ! ' Some of the great men of the past did the same, but that is no justification for us ; we know why they had to do so.

We will now go back to the ordinary man and his religion—the only religion that ought to bear the name. The well-known words of one of our great and wise poets come to mind in which he expresses his view of the relation of religion to art and science. They run :

> He who has Science and has Art,
>   Religion, too, has he ;
> Who has not Science, has not Art,
>   Let him religious be ! [1]

On the one hand, these words contrast religion with the two highest achievements of man, and on the other, they declare that in respect of their value in life they can represent or replace each

[1] Goethe, *Zahmen Xenien IX* (Gedichte aus dem Nachlass).

other.   If we wish to deprive even the ordinary
man, too, of his religion, we shall clearly not have
the authority of the poet on our side.   We will seek
to get in touch with the meaning of his utterance
by a special way.   Life as we find it is too hard
for us ; it entails too much pain, too many disappointments, impossible tasks.   We cannot do
without palliative remedies.   We cannot dispense
with auxiliary constructions, as Theodor Fontane
said.   There are perhaps three of these means :
powerful diversions of interest, which lead us to
care little about our misery ; substitutive gratifications, which lessen it ; and intoxicating substances, which make us insensitive to it.   Something of this kind is indispensable.[1] Voltaire is
aiming at a diversion of interest when he brings his
Candide to a close with the advice that people
should cultivate their gardens ; scientific work is
another deflection of the same kind.   The substitute gratifications, such as art offers, are illusions in contrast to reality, but none the less
satisfying to the mind on that account, thanks to
the place which phantasy has reserved for herself
in mental life.   The intoxicating substances affect
our body, alter its chemical processes.   It is not

[1] Wilhelm Busch, in *Die fromme Helene*, says the same
thing on a lower level : ' The man who has cares has brandy
too.'

so simple to find the place where religion belongs in this series. We must look further afield.

The question, ' What is the purpose of human life ? ' has been asked times without number ; it has never received a satisfactory answer ; perhaps it does not admit of such an answer. Many a questioner has added that if it should appear that life has no purpose, then it would lose all value for him. But these threats alter nothing. It looks, on the contrary, as though one had a right to dismiss this question, for it seems to presuppose that belief in the superiority of the human race with which we are already so familiar in its other expressions. Nobody asks what is the purpose of the lives of animals, unless peradventure they are designed to be of service to man. But this, too, will not hold, for with many animals man can do nothing—except describe, classify and study them ; and countless species have declined to be put even to this use, by living and dying and becoming extinct before men had set eyes upon them. So again, only religion is able to answer the question of the purpose of life. One can hardly go wrong in concluding that the idea of a purpose in life stands and falls with the religious system.

We will turn, therefore, to the less ambitious problem, what the behaviour of men themselves reveals as the purpose and object of their lives, what they demand of life and wish to attain in it. The answer to this can hardly be in doubt : they seek happiness, they want to become happy and to remain so.   There are two sides to this striving, a positive and a negative ; it aims on the one hand at eliminating pain and discomfort, on the other at the experience of intense pleasures. In its narrower sense the word ' happiness ' relates only to the last.   Thus human activities branch off in two directions—corresponding to this double goal —according to which of the two they aim at realizing, either predominantly or even exclusively.

As we see, it is simply the pleasure-principle which draws up the programme of life's purpose. This principle dominates the operation of the mental apparatus from the very beginning ; there can be no doubt about its efficiency, and yet its programme is in conflict with the whole world, with the macrocosm as much as with the microcosm. It simply cannot be put into execution, the whole constitution of things runs counter to it ; one might say the intention that man should be 'happy' is not included in the scheme of ' Creation '.   What is called happiness in its narrowest sense comes from the satisfaction—most often instantaneous—of pent-up needs which have reached great intensity, and by its very nature can only be a transitory experience. When any condition desired by the pleasure-principle is protracted, it results in a feeling only of mild comfort ; we are so constituted that we can only intensely enjoy contrasts, much less intensely states in themselves.[1] Our possibilities of happiness are thus limited from the start by our very constitution. It is much less difficult to be unhappy. Suffering comes from three quarters : from our own body, which is destined to decay and dissolution, and cannot even dispense with anxiety and pain as danger-signals ; from the outer world, which can rage against us with the most powerful and pitiless forces of destruction ; and finally from our relations with other men. The unhappiness which has this last origin we find perhaps more painful than any other ; we tend to regard it more or less as a gratuitous addition, although it cannot be any less an inevitable fate than the suffering that proceeds from other sources.

It is no wonder if, under the pressure of these possibilities of suffering, humanity is wont to reduce its demands for happiness, just as even the pleasure-principle itself changes into the more

[1] Goethe even warns us that ' nothing is so hard to bear as a train of happy days '. This may be an exaggeration all the same.

accommodating reality-principle under the influence of external environment ; if a man thinks himself happy if he has merely escaped unhappiness or weathered trouble ; if in general the task of avoiding pain forces that of obtaining pleasure into the background.   Reflection shows that there are very different ways of attempting to perform this task ; and all these ways have been recommended by the various schools of wisdom in the art of life and put into practice by men.   Unbridled gratification of all desires forces itself into the foreground as the most alluring guiding principle in life, but it entails preferring enjoyment to caution and penalizes itself after short indulgence.   The other methods, in which avoidance of pain is the main motive, are differentiated according to the source of the suffering against which they are mainly directed.   Some of these measures are extreme and some moderate, some are one-sided and some deal with several aspects of the matter at once.   Voluntary loneliness, isolation from others, is the readiest safeguard against the unhappiness that may arise out of human relations.   We know what this means : the happiness found along this path is that of peace. Against the dreaded outer world one can defend oneself only by turning away in some other direction, if the difficulty is to be solved single-handed.

There is indeed another and a better way : that of combining with the rest of the human community and taking up the attack on nature, thus forcing it to obey human will, under the guidance of science.   One is working then with all for the good of all.   But the most interesting methods for averting pain are those which aim at influencing the organism itself.   In the last analysis all pain is but sensation ; it only exists in so far as we feel it, and we feel it only in consequence of certain characteristics of our organism.

The crudest of these methods of influencing the body, but also the most effective, is the chemical one : that of intoxication.   I do not think anyone entirely understands their operation, but it is a fact that there are certain substances foreign to the body which, when present in the blood or tissues, directly cause us pleasurable sensations, but also so change the conditions of our perceptivity that we become insensible of disagreeable sensations.   The two effects not only take place simultaneously, they seem to be closely bound up with each other.   But there must be substances in the chemical composition of our bodies which can do the same, for we know of at least one morbid state, that of mania, in which a condition similar to this intoxication arises without any drug being absorbed.   Besides this, our normal mental life shows variations, according to which pleasure is experienced with more or less ease, and along with this goes a diminished or increased sensitivity to pain.   It is greatly to be regretted that this toxic aspect of mental processes has so far eluded scientific research.   The services rendered by intoxicating substances in the struggle for happiness and in warding off misery rank so highly as a benefit that both individuals and races have given them an established position within their libido-economy.   It is not merely the immediate gain in pleasure which one owes to them, but also a measure of that independence of the outer world which is so sorely craved.   Men know that with the help they can get from ' drowning their cares ' they can at any time slip away from the oppression of reality and find a refuge in a world of their own where painful feelings do not enter.   We are aware that it is just this property which constitutes the danger and injuriousness of intoxicating substances. In certain circumstances they are to blame when valuable energies which could have been used to improve the lot of humanity are uselessly wasted.

The complicated structure of our mental apparatus admits, however, of a whole series of other kinds of influence.   The gratification of

instincts is happiness, but when the outer world
lets us starve, refuses us satisfaction of our needs,
they become the cause of very great suffering.   So
the hope is born that by influencing these impulses
one may escape some measure of suffering.   This
type of defence against pain no longer relates to the
sensory apparatus ; it seeks to control the internal
sources of our needs themselves.   An extreme form
of it consists in annihilation of the instincts, as
taught by the wisdom of the East and practised by
the Yogi.   When it succeeds, it is true, it involves
giving up all other activities as well (sacrificing the
whole of life), and again, by another path, the only
happiness it brings is that of peace.   The same way
is taken when the aim is less extreme and only
control of the instincts is sought.   When this is so,
the higher mental systems which recognize the
reality-principle have the upper hand.   The aim of
gratification is by no means abandoned in this case ;
a certain degree of protection against suffering is
secured, in that lack of satisfaction causes less pain
when the instincts are kept in check than when they
are unbridled.   On the other hand, this brings with
it an undeniable reduction in the degree of enjoyment obtainable.   The feeling of happiness produced by indulgence of a wild, untamed craving is
incomparably more intense than is the satisfying of

a curbed desire. The irresistibility of perverted impulses, perhaps the charm of forbidden things generally, may in this way be explained economically.

Another method of guarding against pain is by using the libido-displacements that our mental equipment allows of, by which it gains so greatly in flexibility. The task is then one of transferring the instinctual aims into such directions that they cannot be frustrated by the outer world. Sublimation of the instincts lends an aid in this. Its success is greatest when a man knows how to heighten sufficiently his capacity for obtaining pleasure from mental and intellectual work. Fate has little power against him then. This kind of satisfaction, such as the artist's joy in creation, in embodying his phantasies, or the scientist's in solving problems or discovering truth, has a special quality which we shall certainly one day be able to define metapsychologically. Until then we can only say metaphorically it seems to us ' higher and finer ', but compared with that of gratifying gross primitive instincts, its intensity is tempered and diffused ; it does not overwhelm us physically. The weak point of this method, however, is that it is not generally applicable ; it is only available to the few. It presupposes special gifts and dis-

positions which are not very commonly found in a
sufficient degree.   And even to these few it does
not secure complete protection against suffering ;
it gives no invulnerable armour against the
arrows of fate, and it usually fails when a
man's own body becomes a source of suffering to
him.[1]

This behaviour reveals clearly enough its aim—
that of making oneself independent of the external
world, by looking for happiness in the inner things
of the mind ; in the next method the same features are even more marked.   The connection
with reality is looser still ; satisfaction is obtained
through illusions, which are recognized as such,
without the discrepancy between them and reality
being allowed to interfere with the pleasure they
give.   These illusions are derived from the life of
phantasy which, at the time when the sense of
reality developed, was expressly exempted from the
demands of the reality-test and set apart for the
purpose of fulfilling wishes which would be very
hard to realize.   At the head of these phantasy-
pleasures stands the enjoyment of works of art

[1] When there is no special disposition in a man imperatively
prescribing the direction of his life-interest, the ordinary work
all can do for a livelihood can play the part which Voltaire wisely
advocated it should do in our lives.   It is not possible to discuss
the significance of work for the economics of the libido adequately
within the limits of a short survey.   Laying stress upon import-

which through the agency of the artist is opened to those who cannot themselves create.[1] Those who are sensitive to the influence of art do not know how to rate it high enough as a source of happiness and consolation in life. Yet art affects us but as a mild narcotic and can provide no more than a temporary refuge for us from the hardships of life ; its influence is not strong enough to make us forget real misery.

Another method operates more energetically and thoroughly ; it regards reality as the source of all suffering, as the one and only enemy, with whom life is intolerable and with whom therefore

---

ance of work has a greater effect than any other technique of living in the direction of binding the individual more closely to reality ; in his work he is at least securely attached to a part of reality, the human community. Work is no less valuable for the opportunity it and the human relations connected with it provide for a very considerable discharge of libidinal component impulses, narcissistic, aggressive and even erotic, than because it is indispensable for subsistence and justifies existence in a society. The daily work of earning a livelihood affords particular satisfaction when it has been selected by free choice, *i.e.* when through sublimation it enables use to be made of existing inclinations, of instinctual impulses that have retained their strength, or are more intense than usual for constitutional reasons. And yet as a path to happiness work is not valued very highly by men. They do not run after it as they do after other opportunities for gratification. The great majority work only when forced by necessity, and this natural human aversion to work gives rise to the most difficult social problems.

[1] Cf. ' Formulations regarding the Two Principles in Mental Functioning ' (1911), *Collected Papers*, vol. iv. ; and *Introductory Lectures on Psycho-Analysis* (1915–17), London, 1922, chapter xxiii.

all relations must be broken off if one is to be happy in any way at all. The hermit turns his back on this world ; he will have nothing to do with it. But one can do more than that ; one can try to re-create it, try to build up another instead, from which the most unbearable features are eliminated and replaced by others corresponding to one's own wishes. He who in his despair and defiance sets out on this path will not as a rule get very far ; reality will be too strong for him. He becomes a madman and usually finds no one to help him in carrying through his delusion. It is said, however, that each one of us behaves in some respect like the paranoiac, substituting a wish-fulfilment for some aspect of the world which is unbearable to him, and carrying this delusion through into reality. When a large number of people make this attempt together and try to obtain assurance of happiness and protection from suffering by a delusional transformation of reality it acquires special significance. The religions of humanity, too, must be classified as mass-delusions of this kind. Needless to say, no one who shares a delusion recognizes it as such.

I do not suppose that I have enumerated all the methods by which men strive to win happiness and keep suffering at bay, and I know, too, that the material might have been arranged differently. One of these methods I have not yet mentioned at all—not because I had forgotten it, but because it will interest us in another connection. How would it be possible to forget this way of all others of practising the art of life ! It is conspicuous for its remarkable capacity to combine characteristic features. Needless to say, it, too, strives to bring about independence of fate—as we may best call it—and with this object it looks for satisfaction within the mind, and uses the capacity for displacing libido which we mentioned before, but it does not turn away from the outer world ; on the contrary, it takes a firm hold of its objects and obtains happiness from an emotional relation to them. Nor is it content to strive for avoidance of pain—that goal of weary resignation ; rather it passes that by heedlessly and holds fast to the deep-rooted, passionate striving for a positive fulfilment of happiness. Perhaps it really comes nearer to this goal than any other method. I am speaking, of course, of that way of life which makes love the centre of all things and anticipates all happiness from loving and being loved. This attitude is familiar enough to all of us ; one of the forms in which love manifests itself, sexual love, gives us our most intense experience of an overwhelming pleasurable sensation and so furnishes a prototype for our strivings after happiness. What is more natural than that we should persist in seeking happiness along the path by which we first encountered it ? The weak side of this way of living is clearly evident ; and were it not for this, no human being would ever have thought of abandoning this path to happiness in favour of any other. We are never so defenceless against suffering as when we love, never so forlornly unhappy as when we have lost our love-object or its love. But this does not complete the story of that way of life which bases happiness on love ; there is much more to be said about it.

We may here go on to consider the interesting case in which happiness in life is sought first and foremost in the enjoyment of beauty, wherever it is to be found by our senses and our judgement, the beauty of human forms and movements, of natural objects, of landscapes, of artistic and even scientific creations. As a goal in life this aesthetic attitude offers little protection against the menace of suffering, but it is able to compensate for a great deal. The enjoyment of beauty produces a particular, mildly intoxicating kind of sensation. There is no very evident use in beauty ; the necessity of it for cultural purposes is not apparent, and yet civilization could not do without it.   The science of aesthetics investigates the conditions in which things are regarded as beautiful ; it can give no explanation of the nature or origin of beauty ; as usual, its lack of results is concealed under a flood of resounding and meaningless words. Unfortunately, psycho-analysis, too, has less to say about beauty than about most things.   Its derivation from the realms of sexual sensation is all that seems certain ; the love of beauty is a perfect example of a feeling with an inhibited aim. ' Beauty ' and ' attraction ' are first of all the attributes of a sexual object.   It is remarkable that the genitals themselves, the sight of which is always exciting, are hardly ever regarded as beautiful ; the quality of beauty seems, on the other hand, to attach to certain secondary sexual characters.

In spite of the incompleteness of these considerations, I will venture on a few remarks in conclusion of this discussion.   The goal towards which the pleasure-principle impels us—of becoming happy—is not attainable ; yet we may not —nay, cannot— give up the effort to come nearer to realization of it by some means or other.   Very different paths may be taken towards it : some pursue the positive aspect of the aim, attainment of pleasure ; others the negative, avoidance of

pain. By none of these ways can we achieve all
that we desire. In that modified sense in which
we have seen it to be attainable, happiness is a
problem of the economics of the libido in each
individual. There is no sovereign recipe in this
matter which suits all ; each one must find out
for himself by which particular means he may
achieve felicity. All kinds of different factors
will operate to influence his choice. It depends
on how much real gratification he is likely to
obtain in the external world, and how far he will
find it necessary to make himself independent of
it ; finally, too, on the belief he has in himself of
his power to alter it in accordance with his wishes.
Even at this stage the mental constitution of the
individual will play a decisive part, aside from any
external considerations. The man who is predominantly erotic will choose emotional relationships with others before all else ; the narcissistic
type, who is more self-sufficient, will seek his
essential satisfactions in the inner workings of his
own soul ; the man of action will never abandon
the external world in which he can essay his
power. The interests of narcissistic types will be
determined by their particular gifts and the
degree of instinctual sublimation of which they are
capable. When any choice is pursued to an

extreme it penalizes itself, in that it exposes the individual to the dangers accompanying any one exclusive life-interest which may always prove inadequate.   Just as a cautious business-man avoids investing all his capital in one concern, so wisdom would probably admonish us also not to anticipate all our happiness from one quarter alone. Success is never certain ; it depends on the co-operation of many factors, perhaps on none more than the capacity of the mental constitution to adapt itself to the outer world and then utilize this last for obtaining pleasure.   Anyone who is born with a specially unfavourable instinctual constitution, and whose libido-components do not go through the transformation and modification necessary for successful achievement in later life, will find it hard to obtain happiness from his external environment, especially if he is faced with the more difficult tasks.   One last possibility of dealing with life remains to such people and it offers them at least substitute-gratifications ; it takes the form of the flight into neurotic illness, and they mostly adopt it while they are still young.   Those whose efforts to obtain happiness come to nought in later years still find consolation in the pleasure of chronic intoxication, or else they embark upon that despairing attempt at revolt—psychosis.

Religion circumscribes these measures of choice and adaptation by urging upon everyone alike its single way of achieving happiness and guarding against pain.   Its method consists in decrying the value of life and promulgating a view of the real world that is distorted like a delusion, and both of these imply a preliminary intimidating influence upon intelligence.   At such a cost—by the forcible imposition of mental infantilism and inducing a mass-delusion—religion succeeds in saving many people from individual neuroses.   But little more. There are, as we have said, many paths by which the happiness attainable for man can be reached, but none which is certain to take him to it.   Nor can religion keep her promises either.   When the faithful find themselves reduced in the end to speaking of God's ' inscrutable decree ', they thereby avow that all that is left to them in their sufferings is unconditional submission as a last-remaining consolation and source of happiness. And if a man is willing to come to this, he could probably have arrived there by a shorter road.

III

OUR discussion of happiness has so far not taught us much that is not already common knowledge. Nor does the prospect of discovering anything new seem much greater if we go on with the problem why it is so hard for mankind to be happy. We gave the answer before, when we cited the three sources of human sufferings, namely, the superior force of nature, the disposition to decay of our bodies, and the inadequacy of our methods of regulating human relations in the family, the community and the state. In regard to the first two, our judgement cannot hesitate : it forces us to recognize these sources of suffering and to submit to the inevitable. We shall never completely subdue nature ; our body, too, is an organism, itself a part of nature, and will always contain the seeds of dissolution, with its limited powers of adaptation and achievement. The effect of this recognition is in no way disheartening ; on the contrary, it points out the direction for our efforts. If we cannot abolish all suffering, yet a great deal of it we can, and can mitigate more ; the experience of several thousand years has convinced us of this. To the third, the social source of our distresses, we take up a different attitude. We prefer not to regard it as one at all ; we cannot see why the systems we have ourselves created should not rather ensure protection and well-being for us all. To be sure, when we consider how unsuccessful our efforts to safeguard against suffering in this particular have proved, the suspicion dawns upon us that a bit of unconquerable nature lurks concealed behind this difficulty as well—in the shape of our own mental constitution.

When we start to consider this possibility, we come across a point of view which is so amazing that we will pause over it. According to it, our so-called civilization itself is to blame for a great part of our misery, and we should be much happier if we were to give it up and go back to primitive conditions. I call this amazing because—however one may define culture—it is undeniable that every means by which we try to guard ourselves against menaces from the several sources of human distress is a part of this same culture.

How has it come about that so many people have adopted this strange attitude of hostility to civilization ? In my opinion, it arose from a background of profound long-standing discontent with the existing state of civilization, which finally crystallized into this judgement as a result of certain historical happenings. I believe I can identify the last two of these ; I am not learned enough to trace the links in the chain back into the history of the human species. At the time when Christianity conquered the pagan religions some such antagonism to culture must already have been actively at work. It is closely related to the low estimation put upon earthly life by Christian doctrine. The earlier of the last two historical developments was when, as a result of voyages of discovery, men came into contact with primitive peoples and races. To the Europeans, who failed to observe them carefully and misunderstood what they saw, these people seemed to lead simple, happy lives—wanting for nothing—such as the travellers who visited them, with all their superior culture, were unable to achieve. Later experience has corrected this opinion on many points ; in several instances the ease of life was due to the bounty of nature and the possibilities of ready satisfaction for the great human needs, but it was erroneously attributed to the absence of the complicated conditions of civilization. The last of the two historical events is especially familiar to us ; it was when people began to understand the nature of the neuroses which threaten to undermine the modicum of happiness open to civilized man. It was found that men become neurotic because they cannot tolerate the degree of privation that society imposes on them in virtue of its cultural ideals, and it was supposed that a return to greater possibilities of happiness would ensue if these standards were abolished or greatly relaxed.

And there exists an element of disappointment, in addition. In the last generations man has made extraordinary strides in knowledge of the natural sciences and technical application of them, and has established his dominion over nature in a way never before imagined. The details of this forward progress are universally known : it is unnecessary to enumerate them. Mankind is proud of its exploits and has a right to be. But men are beginning to perceive that all this newly-won power over space and time, this conquest of the forces of nature, this fulfilment of age-old longings, has not increased the amount of pleasure they can obtain in life, has not made them feel any happier. The valid conclusion from this is merely that power over nature is not the only condition of human happiness, just as it is not the only goal of civilization's efforts, and there is no ground for inferring that its technical progress is worthless from the standpoint of happiness. It prompts one to exclaim : is it not then a positive pleasure, an unequivocal gain in happiness, to be able to hear, whenever I like, the voice of a child living hundreds of miles away, or to know directly a friend of mine arrives at his destination that he has come well and safely through the long and troublesome voyage ? And is it nothing that medical science has succeeded in enormously reducing the mortality of young children, the dangers of infection for women in childbirth, indeed, in very considerably prolonging the average length of human life ? And there is still a long list one could add to these benefits that we owe to the much-despised era of scientific and practical progress—but a critical, pessimistic voice makes itself heard, saying that most of these advantages follow the model of those ' cheap pleasures ' in the anecdote. One gets this enjoyment by sticking one's bare leg outside the bedclothes on a cold winter's night and then drawing it in again. If there were no railway to make light of distances my child would never have left home and I should not need the telephone to hear his voice. If there were no vessels crossing the ocean my friend would never have embarked on his voyage and I should not need the telegraph to relieve my anxiety about him.   What is the use of reducing the mortality of children when it is precisely this reduction which imposes the greatest moderation on us in begetting them, so that taken all round we do not rear more children than in the days before the reign of hygiene, while at the same time we have created difficult conditions for sexual life in marriage and probably counteracted the beneficial effects of natural selection ?   And what do we gain by a long life when it is full of hardship and starved of joys and so wretched that we can only welcome death as our deliverer ?

It seems to be certain that our present-day civilization does not inspire in us a feeling of well-being, but it is very difficult to form an opinion whether in earlier times people felt any happier and what part their cultural conditions played in the question.   We always tend to regard trouble objectively, *i.e.* to place ourselves with our own wants and our own sensibilities in the same conditions, so as to discover what opportunities for happiness or unhappiness we should find in them. This method of considering the problem, which appears to be objective because it ignores the varieties of subjective sensitivity, is of course the most subjective possible, for by applying it one substitutes one's own mental attitude for the unknown attitude of other men.   Happiness, on the contrary, is something essentially subjective.   However we may shrink in horror at the thought of certain situations, that of the galley-slaves in antiquity, of the peasants in the Thirty Years' War, of the victims of the Inquisition, of the Jews awaiting a pogrom, it is still impossible for us to feel ourselves into the position of these people, to imagine the differences which would be brought about by constitutional obtuseness of feeling, gradual stupefaction, the cessation of all anticipation, and by all the grosser and more subtle ways in which insensibility to both pleasurable and painful sensations can be induced.   Moreover, on occasions when the most extreme forms of suffering have to be endured, special mental protective devices come into operation.   It seems to me unprofitable to follow up this aspect of the problem further.

It is time that we should turn our attention to the nature of this culture, the value of which is so much disputed from the point of view of happiness. Until we have learnt something by examining it for ourselves, we will not look round for formulas which express its essence in a few words.   We will be content to repeat [1] that the word ' culture ' describes the sum of the achievements and institu-

[1] Cf. *The Future of an Illusion.*

tions which differentiate our lives from those of our animal forebears and serve two purposes, namely, that of protecting humanity against nature and of regulating the relations of human beings among themselves. In order to learn more than this, we must bring together the individual features of culture as they are manifested in human communities. We shall have no hesitation in allowing ourselves to be guided by the common usages of language, or as one might say, the *feeling* of language, confident that we shall thus take into account inner attitudes which still resist expression in abstract terms.

The beginning is easy. We recognize as belonging to culture all the activities and possessions which men use to make the earth serviceable to them, to protect them against the tyranny of natural forces, and so on. There is less doubt about this aspect of civilization than any other. If we go back far enough we find that the first acts of civilization were the use of tools, the gaining of power over fire, and the construction of dwellings. Among these the acquisition of power over fire stands out as a quite exceptional achievement, without a prototype ; [1] while the other two opened up paths

[1] Psycho-analytic material, as yet incomplete and not capable of unequivocal interpretation, nevertheless admits of a surmise—which sounds fantastic enough—about the origin of this human

which have ever since been pursued by man, the stimulus towards which is easily imágined. By means of all his tools, man makes his own organs more perfect—both the motor and the sensory— or else removes the obstacles in the way of their activity. Machinery places gigantic power at his disposal which, like his muscles, he can employ in any direction ; ships and aircraft have the effect that neither air nor water can prevent his travers- ing them. With spectacles he corrects the defects of the lens in his own eyes ; with telescopes he looks at far distances ; with the microscope he overcomes the limitations in visibility due to the structure of his retina. With the photographic

---

feat. It is as if primitive man had had the impulse, when he came in contact with fire, to gratify an infantile pleasure in respect of it and put it out with a stream of urine. The legends that we possess leave no doubt that flames shooting upwards like tongues were originally felt to have a phallic sense. Putting out fire by urinating—which is also introduced in the later fables of Gulliver in Lilliput and Rabelais's Gargantua—therefore repre- sented a sexual act with a man, an enjoyment of masculine potency in homosexual rivalry. Whoever was the first to deny himself this pleasure and spare the fire was able to take it with him and break it in to his own service. By curbing the fire of his own sexual passion he was able to tame fire as a force of nature. This great cultural victory was thus a reward for refraining from gratification of an instinct. Further, it is as if man had placed woman by the hearth as the guardian of the fire he had taken captive, because her anatomy makes it impossible for her to yield to such a temptation. It is remarkable how regularly analytic findings testify to the close connection between the ideas of ambition, fire and urethral erotism.

camera he has created an instrument which registers transitory visual impressions, just as the gramophone does with equally transient auditory ones ; both are at bottom materializations of his own power of memory. With the help of the telephone he can hear at distances which even fairytales would treat as insuperable ; writing to begin with was the voice of the absent ; dwellings were a substitute for the mother's womb, that first abode, in which he was safe and felt so content, for which he probably yearns ever after.

It sounds like a fairy-tale, but not only that ; this story of what man by his science and practical inventions has achieved on this earth, where he first appeared as a weakly member of the animal kingdom, and on which each individual of his species must ever again appear as a helpless infant —O inch of nature !—is a direct fulfilment of all, or of most, of the dearest wishes in his fairy-tales. All these possessions he has acquired through culture. Long ago he formed an ideal conception of omnipotence and omniscience which he embodied in his gods. Whatever seemed unattainable to his desires—or forbidden to him—he attributed to these gods. One may say, therefore, that these gods were the ideals of his culture. Now he has himself approached very near to realizing this ideal, he has nearly become a god himself. But only, it is true, in the way that ideals are usually realized in the general experience of humanity. Not completely ; in some respects not at all, in others only by halves. Man has become a god by means of artificial limbs, so to speak, quite magnificent when equipped with all his accessory organs ; but they do not grow on him and they still give him trouble at times. However, he is entitled to console himself with the thought that this evolution will not come to an end in A.D. 1930. Future ages will produce further great advances in this realm of culture, probably inconceivable now, and will increase man's likeness to a god still more. But with the aim of our study in mind, we will not forget, all the same, that the human being of to-day is not happy with all his likeness to a god.

Thus we recognize that a country has attained a high level of civilization when we find that everything in it that can be helpful in exploiting the earth for man's benefit and in protecting him against nature—everything, in short, that is useful to him—is cultivated and effectively protected. In such a country the course of rivers which threaten to overflow their banks is regulated, their waters guided through canals to places where they are needed. The soil is industriously cultivated and planted with the vegetation suited to it ; the mineral wealth is brought up assiduously from the depths and wrought into the implements and utensils that are required. The means of communication are frequent, rapid and reliable ; wild and dangerous animals have been exterminated, the breeding of tamed and domesticated ones prospers. But we demand other things besides these of civilization, and, curiously enough, we expect to find them existing in the same countries. As if we wished to repudiate the first requisition we made, we count it also as proof of a high level of civilization when we see that the industry of the inhabitants is applied as well to things which are not in the least useful and, on the contrary, seem to be useless, *e.g.* when the parks and gardens in a town, which are necessary as playgrounds and air-reservoirs, also bear flowering plants, or when the windows of dwellings are adorned with flowers. We soon become aware that the useless thing which we require of civilization is beauty ; we expect a cultured people to revere beauty where it is found in nature and to create it in their handiwork so far as they are able. But this is far from exhausting what we require of civilization. Besides, we expect to see the signs

of cleanliness and order. We do not think highly
of the cultural level of an English country town
in the time of Shakespeare when we read that
there was a tall dungheap in front of his father's
house in Stratford ; we are indignant and call it
' barbarous ', which is the opposite of civilized,
when we find the paths in the Wiener Wald
littered with paper. Dirt of any kind seems to us
incompatible with civilization ; we extend our
demands for cleanliness to the human body also,
and are amazed to hear what an objectionable
odour emanated from the person of the Roi
Soleil ; we shake our heads when we are shown
the tiny wash-basin on the Isola Bella which
Napoleon used for his daily ablutions. Indeed,
we are not surprised if anyone employs the use of
soap as a direct measure of civilization. It is the
same with order, which, like cleanliness, relates
entirely to man's handiwork. But whereas we
cannot expect cleanliness in nature, order has, on
the contrary, been imitated from nature ; man's
observations of the great astronomical periodicities
not only furnished him with a model, but formed
the ground-plan of his first attempts to introduce
order into his own life. Order is a kind of repetition-compulsion by which it is ordained once for
all when, where and how a thing shall be done so

that on every similar occasion doubt and hesitation shall be avoided. The benefits of order are incontestable : it enables us to use space and time to the best advantage, while saving expenditure of mental energy. One would be justified in expecting that it would have ingrained itself from the start and without opposition into all human activities; and one may well wonder that this has not happened, and that, on the contrary, human beings manifest an inborn tendency to negligence, irregularity and untrustworthiness in their work, and have to be laboriously trained to imitate the example of their celestial models.

Beauty, cleanliness and order clearly occupy a peculiar position among the requirements of civilization. No one will maintain that they are as essential to life as the activities aimed at controlling the forces of nature and as other factors which we have yet to mention ; and yet no one would willingly relegate them to the background as trivial matters. Beauty is an instance which plainly shows that culture is not simply utilitarian in its aims, for the lack of beauty is a thing we cannot tolerate in civilization. The utilitarian advantages of order are quite apparent ; with regard to cleanliness we have to remember that it is required of us by hygiene, and we may surmise that even before the days of scientific prophylaxis the connection between the two was not altogether unsuspected by mankind. But these aims and endeavours of culture are not entirely to be explained on utilitarian lines ; there must be something else at work besides.

According to general opinion, however, there is one feature of culture which characterizes it better than any other, and that is the value it sets upon the higher mental activities—intellectual, scientific, and aesthetic achievement—the leading part it concedes to ideas in human life. First and foremost among these ideas come the religious systems with their complicated evolution, on which I have elsewhere endeavoured to throw a light ; next to them come philosophical speculations ; and last, the ideals man has formed, his conceptions of the perfection possible in an individual, in a people, in humanity as a whole, and the demands he makes on the basis of these conceptions. These creations of his mind are not independent of each other ; on the contrary, they are closely interwoven, and this complicates the attempt to describe them, as well as that to trace their psychological derivation. If we assume as a general hypothesis that the force behind all human activities is a striving towards the two convergent aims of profit and pleasure, we must then acknowledge this as valid also for these other manifestations of culture, although it can be plainly recognized as true only in respect of science and art. It cannot be doubted, however, that the remainder, too, correspond to some powerful need in human beings— perhaps to one which develops fully only in a minority of people. Nor may we allow ourselves to be misled by our own judgements concerning the value of any of these religious or philosophical systems or of these ideals ; whether we look upon them as the highest achievement of the human mind, or whether we deplore them as fallacies, one must acknowledge that where they exist, and especially where they are in the ascendant, they testify to a high level of civilization.

We now have to consider the last, and certainly by no means the least important, of the components of culture, namely, the ways in which social relations, the relations of one man to another, are regulated, all that has to do with him as a neighbour, a source of help, a sexual object to others, a member of a family or of a state. It is especially difficult in this matter to remain unbiased by any ideal standards and to ascertain exactly what is specifically cultural here. Perhaps one might begin with the statement that the first attempt ever made to regulate these social relations already contained the essential element of civilization. Had no such attempt been made, these relations would be subject to the wills of individuals : that is to say, the man who was physically strongest would decide things in accordance with his own interests and desires. The situation would remain the same even though this strong man should in his turn meet with another who was stronger than he. Human life in communities only becomes possible when a number of men unite together in strength superior to any single individual and remain united against all single individuals. The strength of this united body is then opposed as ' Right ' against the strength of any individual, which is condemned as ' brute force '. This substitution of the power of a united number for the power of a single man is the decisive step towards civilization. The essence of it lies in the circumstance that the members of the community have restricted their possibilities of gratification, whereas the individual recognized no such restrictions. The first requisite of culture, therefore, is justice—that is, the assurance that a law once made will not be broken in favour of any individual. This implies nothing about the ethical value of any such law. The further course of cultural development seems to tend towards

ensuring that the law shall no longer represent the
will of any small body—caste, tribe, section of the
population—which may behave like a predatory
individual towards other such groups perhaps con-
taining larger numbers.   The end-result would be
a state of law to which all—that is, all who are
capable of uniting—have contributed by making
some sacrifice of their own desires, and which leaves
none—again with the same exception—at the
mercy of brute force.

The liberty of the individual is not a benefit of
culture. It was greatest before any culture, though
indeed it had little value at that time, because the
individual was hardly in a position to defend it.
Liberty has undergone restrictions through the
evolution of civilization and justice demands that
these restrictions shall apply to all.   The desire for
freedom that makes itself felt in a human community may be a revolt against some existing
injustice and so may prove favourable to a further
development of civilization and remain compatible
with it.   But it may also have its origin in the
primitive roots of the personality, still unfettered
by civilizing influences, and so become a source of
antagonism to culture.   Thus the cry for freedom
is directed either against particular forms or
demands of culture or else against culture itself.

It does not seem as if man could be brought by any sort of influence to change his nature into that of the ants ; he will always, one imagines, defend his claim to individual freedom against the will of the multitude.   A great part of the struggles of mankind centres round the single task of finding some expedient (*i.e.* satisfying) solution between these individual claims and those of the civilized community ; it is one of the problems of man's fate whether this solution can be arrived at in some particular form of culture or whether the conflict will prove irreconcilable.

We have obtained a clear impression of the general picture presented by culture through adopting the common view as to which aspects of human life are to be called cultural ; but it is true that so far we have discovered nothing that is not common knowledge.   We have, however, at the same time guarded ourselves against accepting the misconception that civilization is synonymous with becoming perfect, is the path by which man is ordained to reach perfection.   But now a certain point of view presses for consideration ; it will lead perhaps in another direction.   The evolution of culture seems to us a peculiar kind of process passing over humanity, of which several aspects strike us as familiar.   We can describe this process in terms of the modifications it effects on the known human instinctual dispositions, which it is the economic task of our lives to satisfy. Some of these instincts become absorbed, as it were, so that something appears in place of them which in an individual we call a character-trait. The most remarkable example of this process is found in respect of the anal erotism of young human beings. Their primary interest in the excretory function, its organs and products, is changed in the course of their growth into a group of traits that we know well—thriftiness, orderliness and cleanliness— valuable and welcome qualities in themselves, which, however, may be intensified till they visibly dominate the personality and produce what we call the anal character. How this happens we do not know; but there is no doubt about the accuracy of this conclusion.[1] Now, we have seen that order and cleanliness are essentially cultural demands, although the necessity of them for survival is not particularly apparent, any more than their suitability as sources of pleasure. At this point we must be struck for the first time with the similarity between the process of cultural development and that of the libidinal development in an individual.

[1] Cf. ' Character and Anal Erotism ' (1908), *Collected Papers*, vol. ii. ; also numerous contributions to the subject by Ernest Jones and others.

Other instincts have to be induced to change the conditions of their gratification, to find it along other paths, a process which is usually identical with what we know so well as sublimation (of the aim of an instinct), but which can sometimes be differentiated from this. Sublimation of instinct is an especially conspicuous feature of cultural evolution ; this it is that makes it possible for the higher mental operations, scientific, artistic, ideological activities, to play such an important part in civilized life. If one were to yield to a first impression, one would be tempted to say that sublimation is a fate which has been forced upon instincts by culture alone. But it is better to reflect over this a while longer. Thirdly and lastly, and this seems most important of all, it is impossible to ignore the extent to which civilization is built up on renunciation of instinctual gratifications, the degree to which the existence of civilization presupposes the non-gratification (suppression, repression or something else ?) of powerful instinctual urgencies. This ' cultural privation ' dominates the whole field of social relations between human beings ; we know already that it is the cause of the antagonism against which all civilization has to fight. It sets hard tasks for our scientific work, too; we have a great deal to explain here. It is not easy to understand how it can become possible to with-hold satisfaction from an instinct.   Nor is it by any means without risk to do so ; if the deprivation is not made good economically, one may be certain of producing serious disorders.

But now, if we wish to know what use it is to us to have recognized the evolution of culture as a special process, comparable to the normal growth of an individual to maturity, we must clearly attack another problem and put the question : what are the influences to which the evolution of culture owes its origin, how did it arise and what determined its course ?

IV

THIS task seems too big a one ; one may well confess oneself diffident. Here follows what little I have been able to elicit about it.

Once primitive man had made the discovery that it lay in his own hands—speaking literally—to improve his lot on earth by working, it cannot have been a matter of indifference to him whether another man worked with him or against him. The other acquired the value of a fellow-worker, and it was advantageous to live with him. Even earlier, in his ape-like prehistory, man had adopted the habit of forming families : his first helpers were probably the members of his family. One may suppose that the founding of families was in some way connected with the period when the need for genital satisfaction, no longer appearing like an occasional guest who turns up suddenly and then vanishes without letting one hear anything of him for long intervals, had settled down with each man like a permanent lodger. When

E

this happened, the male acquired a motive for keeping the female, or rather, his sexual objects, near him ; while the female, who wanted not to be separated from her helpless young, in their interests, too, had to stay by the stronger male.[1]   In

[1] The organic periodicity of the sexual process has persisted, it is true, but its effect on mental sexual excitation has been almost reversed. This change is connected primarily with the diminishing importance of the olfactory stimuli by means of which the menstrual process produced sexual excitement in the mind of the male. Their function was taken over by visual stimuli, which could operate permanently, instead of intermittently like the olfactory ones. The ' taboo of menstruation ' has its origin in this ' organic repression ', which acted as a barrier against a phase of development that had been surpassed ; all its other motivations are probably of a secondary nature. (Cf. C. D. Daly, ' Hindumythologie und Kastrationskomplex', *Imago*, Bd. xiii., 1927.) This process is repeated on a different level when the gods of a foregone cultural epoch are changed into demons in the next. The diminution in importance of olfactory stimuli seems itself, however, to be a consequence of man's erecting himself from the earth, of his adoption of an upright gait, which made his genitals, that before had been covered, visible and in need of protection and so evoked feelings of shame. Man's erect posture, therefore, would represent the beginning of the momentous process of cultural evolution. The chain of development would run from this onward, through the diminution in the importance of olfactory stimuli and the isolation of women at their periods to a time when visual stimuli became paramount. the genitals became visible, further till sexual excitation became constant and the family was founded, and so to the threshold of human culture. This is only a theoretical speculation, but it is important enough to be worth checking carefully by the conditions obtaining among the animals closely allied to man.

There is an unmistakable social factor at work in the impulse of civilization towards cleanliness, which has been subsequently justified by considerations of hygiene but had nevertheless found expression before they were appreciated. The impulse towards cleanliness originates in the striving to get rid of excretions which

this primitive family one essential feature of culture is lacking ; the will of the father, the head of it, was unfettered. I have endeavoured in *Totem und Tabu* to show how the way led from this family-life to the succeeding phase of communal existence in the form of a band of brothers. By overpowering the father, the sons had discovered that several men united can be stronger than a single man. The totemic stage of culture is

---

have become unpleasant to the sense-perceptions. We know that things are different in the nursery. Excreta arouse no aversion in children ; they seem precious to them, as being parts of their own bodies which have been detached from them. The training of children is very energetic in this particular ; its object is to expedite the development that lies ahead of them, according to which the excreta are to become worthless, disgusting, horrible and despicable to them. Such a reversal of values would be almost impossible to bring about, were it not that these substances expelled from the body are destined by their strong odours to share the fate that overtook the olfactory stimuli after man had erected himself from the ground. Anal erotism, therefore, is from the first subjected to the ' organic repression ' which opened up the way to culture. The social factor which has been active in the further modifications of anal erotism comes into play with the fact that in spite of all man's evolutionary progress the smell of his own excretions is scarcely disagreeable to him yet, but so far only that of the evacuations of others. The man who is not clean, *i.e.* who does not eliminate his excretions, therefore offends others, shows no consideration for them—a fact which is exemplified in the commonest and most forcible terms of abuse. It would be incomprehensible, too, that man should use as an abusive epithet the name of his most faithful friend in the animal world, if dogs did not incur the contempt of men through two of their characteristics, *i.e.* that they are creatures of smell and have no horror of excrement, and, secondly, that they are not ashamed of their sexual functions.

founded upon the restrictions that the band were obliged to impose on one another in order to maintain the new system. These taboos were the first ' Right ' or law. The life of human beings in common therefore had a twofold foundation, *i.e.* the compulsion to work, created by external necessity, and the power of love, causing the male to wish to keep his sexual object, the female, near him, and the female to keep near her that part of herself which has become detached from her, her child. Eros and Ananke were the parents of human culture, too. The first result of culture was that a larger number of human beings could then live together in common. And since the two great powers were here co-operating together, one might have expected that further cultural evolution would have proceeded smoothly towards ever greater mastery over the external world, as well as towards greater extension in the numbers of men sharing the life in common. Nor is it easy to understand how this culture can be felt as anything but satisfying by those who partake of it.

Before we go on to enquire where the disturbances in it arise, we will let ourselves digress from the point that love was one of the founders of culture and so fill a gap left in our previous discussion. We said that man, having found by experience that sexual (genital) love afforded him his greatest gratification, so that it became in effect a prototype of all happiness to him, must have been thereby impelled to seek his happiness further along the path of sexual relations, to make genital erotism the central point of his life. We went on to say that in so doing he becomes to a very dangerous degree dependent on a part of the outer world, namely, on his chosen love-object, and this exposes him to most painful sufferings if he is rejected by it or loses it through death or defection. The wise men of all ages have consequently warned us emphatically against this way of life; but in spite of all it retains its attraction for a great number of people.

A small minority are enabled by their constitution nevertheless to find happiness along the path of love ; but far-reaching mental transformations of the erotic function are necessary before this is possible. These people make themselves independent of their object's acquiescence by transferring the main value from the fact of being loved to their own act of loving ; they protect themselves against loss of it by attaching their love not to individual objects but to all men equally, and they avoid the uncertainties and disappointments of genital love by turning away from its sexual aim and modifying the instinct into an impulse with an *inhibited aim*. The state which they induce in themselves by this process—an unchangeable, undeviating, tender attitude—has little superficial likeness to the stormy vicissitudes of genital love, from which it is nevertheless derived. It seems that Saint Francis of Assisi may have carried this method of using love to produce an inner feeling of happiness as far as anyone ; what we are thus characterizing as one of the procedures by which the pleasure-principle fulfils itself has in fact been linked up in many ways with religion ; the connection between them may lie in those remote fastnesses of the mind where the distinctions between the ego and objects and between the various objects become matters of indifference. From one ethical standpoint, the deeper motivation of which will later become clear to us, this inclination towards an all-embracing love of others and of the world at large is regarded as the highest state of mind of which man is capable. Even at this early stage in the discussion I will not withhold the two principal objections we have to raise against this view. A love that does not discriminate seems to us to lose some of its own value, since it does an injustice to its object. And secondly, not all men are worthy of love.

The love that instituted the family still retains its power; in its original form it does not stop short of direct sexual satisfaction, and in its modified form as aim-inhibited friendliness it influences our civilization. In both these forms it carries on its task of binding men and women to one another, and it does this with greater intensity than can be achieved through the interest of work in common. The casual and undifferentiated way in which the word ' love ' is employed by language has its genetic justification. In general usage the relation between a man and a woman whose genital desires have led them to found a family is called love ; but the positive attitude of feeling between parents and children, between brothers and sisters in a family, is also called love, although to us this relation merits the description of aim-inhibited love or affection. Love with an inhibited aim was indeed originally full sensual love and in men's unconscious minds is so still. Both of them, the sensual and the aim-inhibited forms, reach out beyond the family and create new bonds with others who before were strangers. Genital love leads to the forming of new families ; aim-inhibited love to ' friendships ', which are valuable culturally because they do not

entail many of the limitations of genital love—
for instance, its exclusiveness. But the inter-
relations between love and culture lose their sim-
plicity as development proceeds. On the one
hand, love opposes the interests of culture; on
the other, culture menaces love with grievous restrictions.

This rift between them seems inevitable ; the
cause of it is not immediately recognizable. It
expresses itself first in a conflict between the family
and the larger community to which the individual
belongs. We have seen already that one of culture's principal endeavours is to cement men and
women together into larger units. But the family
will not give up the individual. The closer the
attachment between the members of it, the more
they often tend to remain aloof from others, and
the harder it is for them to enter into the wider
circle of the world at large. That form of life in
common which is phylogenetically older, and is in
childhood its only form, resists being displaced by
the type that becomes acquired later with culture.
Detachment from the family has become a task that
awaits every adolescent, and often society helps
him through it with pubertal and initiatory rites.
One gets the impression that these difficulties form
an integral part of every process of mental evolu-

tion—and indeed, at bottom, of every organic development, too.

The next discord is caused by women, who soon become antithetical to cultural trends and spread around them their conservative influence—the women who at the beginning laid the foundations of culture by the appeal of their love. Women represent the interests of the family and sexual life ; the work of civilization has become more and more men's business ; it confronts them with ever harder tasks, compels them to sublimations of instinct which women are not easily able to achieve. Since man has not an unlimited amount of mental energy at his disposal, he must accomplish his tasks by distributing his libido to the best advantage. What he employs for cultural purposes he withdraws to a great extent from women and his sexual life ; his constant association with men and his dependence on his relations with them even estrange him from his duties as husband and father. Woman finds herself thus forced into the background by the claims of culture and she adopts an inimical attitude towards it.

The tendency of culture to set restrictions upon sexual life is no less evident than its other aim of widening its sphere of operations. Even the earliest phase of it, the totemic, brought in its train the prohibition against incestuous object-choice, perhaps the most maiming wound ever inflicted throughout the ages on the erotic life of man. Further limitations are laid on it by taboos, laws and customs, which touch men as well as women. Various types of culture differ in the lengths to which they carry this ; and the material structure of the social fabric also affects the measure of sexual freedom that remains. We have seen that culture obeys the laws of psychological economic necessity in making the restrictions, for it obtains a great part of the mental energy it needs by subtracting it from sexuality. Culture behaves towards sexuality in this respect like a tribe or a section of the population which has gained the upper hand and is exploiting the rest to its own advantage. Fear of a revolt among the oppressed then becomes a motive for even stricter regulations. A high-water mark in this type of development has been reached in our Western European civilization. Psychologically it is fully justified in beginning by censuring any manifestations of the sexual life of children, for there would be no prospect of curbing the sexual desires of adults if the ground had not been prepared for it in childhood. Nevertheless there is no sort of justification for the lengths beyond this to which civilized society goes in

actually denying the existence of these manifestations, which are not merely demonstrable but posi-
tively glaring.   Where sexually mature persons
are concerned, object-choice is further narrowed
down to the opposite sex and most of the extra-
genital forms of satisfaction are interdicted as
perversions.   The standard which declares itself in
these prohibitions is that of a sexual life identical
for all ; it pays no heed to the disparities in the
inborn and acquired sexual constitutions of individuals and cuts off a considerable number of
them from sexual enjoyment, thus becoming a
cause of grievous injustice.   The effect of these
restrictive measures might presumably be that all
the sexual interest of those who are normal and not
constitutionally handicapped could flow without
further forfeiture into the channel left open to it.
But the only outlet not thus censured, hetero-
sexual genital love, is further circumscribed by the
barriers of legitimacy and monogamy.   Present-
day civilization gives us plainly to understand that
sexual relations are permitted only on the basis
of a final, indissoluble bond between a man and
woman ; that sexuality as a source of enjoyment
for its own sake is unacceptable to it ; and that
its intention is to tolerate it only as the hitherto
irreplaceable means of multiplying the human race.

This, of course, represents an extreme.   Everyone knows that it has proved impossible to put it
into execution, even for short periods.   Only the
weaklings have submitted to such comprehensive
interference with their sexual freedom, and stronger
natures have done so only under one compensatory
condition, of which mention may be made later.
Civilized society has seen itself obliged to pass over
in silence many transgressions which by its own
ordinances it ought to have penalized.   This does
not justify anyone, however, in leaning towards the
other side and assuming that, because it does not
achieve all it aims at, such an attitude on the part
of society is altogether harmless.   The sexual life
of civilized man is seriously disabled, whatever we
may say ; it sometimes makes an impression of
being a function in process of becoming atrophied,
just as organs like our teeth and our hair seem to
be.   One is probably right in supposing that the
importance of sexuality as a source of pleasurable
sensations, *i.e.* as a means of fulfilling the purpose
of life, has perceptibly decreased.[1]   Sometimes one
imagines one perceives that it is not only the
oppression of culture, but something in the nature
of the function itself that denies us full satisfaction

[1] There is a short story, which I valued long ago, by a highly
sensitive writer, the Englishman, John Galsworthy, who to-day

and urges us in other directions.   This may be an
error ; it is hard to decide.[1]

---

enjoys general recognition ; it is called ' The Apple Tree '.   It
shows in a very moving and forcible way how there is no longer
any place in present-day civilized life for a simple natural love
between two human beings.

    [1] The following considerations would support the view ex-
pressed above.   Man, too, is an animal with an unmistakably
bisexual disposition.   The individual represents a fusion of two
symmetrical halves, of which, according to many authorities, one
is purely male, the other female.   It is equally possible that each
half was originally hermaphroditic.   Sex is a biological fact which
is hard to evaluate psychologically, although it is of extraordinary
importance in mental life.   We are accustomed to say that every
human being displays both male and female instinctual impulses,
needs and attributes, but the characteristics of what is male
and female can only be demonstrated in anatomy, and not in
psychology.   Where the latter is concerned, the antithesis of sex
fades away into that of activity and passivity, and we far too
readily identify activity with masculinity and passivity with
femininity, a statement which is by no means universally confirmed
in the animal world.   The theory of bisexuality is still very obscure
and in psycho-analysis we must be painfully aware of the disadvantage we are under as long as it still remains unconnected
with the theory of instincts.   However this may be, if we assume
it to be a fact that each individual has both male and female
desires which need satisfaction in his sexual life, we shall be
prepared for the possibility that these needs will not both be
gratified on the same object, and that they will interfere with
each other, if they cannot be kept apart so that each impulse
flows into a special channel suited for it.   Another difficulty arises
from the circumstance that so often a measure of direct aggressiveness is coupled with an erotic relationship, over and above its
inherent sadistic components.   The love-object does not always
view these complications with the degree of understanding and
tolerance manifested by the peasant woman who complained that
her husband did not love her any more, because he had not beaten
her for a week.

    The conjecture which leads furthest, however, is that—and

here we come back to the remarks in the footnote on p. 66—the whole of sexuality and not merely anal erotism is threatened with falling a victim to the organic repression consequent upon man's adoption of the erect posture and the lowering in value of the sense of smell ; so that since that time the sexual function has been associated with a resistance not susceptible of further explanation, which puts obstacles in the way of full satisfaction and forces it away from its sexual aim towards sublimations and displacements of libido.   I am aware that Bleuler (in ' Der Sexualwiderstand ', *Jahrbuch für psychoanalytische und psychopathologische Forschungen*, Bd. v., 1913) once pointed out the existence of a fundamental tendency of this kind towards rejecting sexual life.   All neurotics, and many others too, take exception to the fact that ' inter urinas et faeces nascimur '.   The genitals, too, excite the olfactory sense strongly in a way that many people cannot tolerate and which spoils sexual intercourse for them. Thus we should find, as the deepest root of the sexual repression that marches with culture, the organic defence of the new form of life that began with the erect posture against the earliest type of animal existence—a result of scientific researches that coincides in a curious way with often expressed vulgar prejudices.   At the present time, nevertheless, these results are but unconfirmed possibilities, not yet scientifically substantiated.   Nor should we forget that, in spite of the undeniable diminution in the importance of olfactory stimuli, there exist even in Europe races who prize highly as aphrodisiacs the strong genital odours so objectionable to us and who will not renounce them. (Cf. the reports of folkloristic information obtained by Iwan Bloch's ' Questionnaire ', appearing under the title of ' Über den Geruchssinn in der vita sexualis ' in various volumes of Friedrich S. Krauss' *Anthropophyteia*.)

V

PSYCHO - ANALYTIC work has shown that these frustrations in respect of sexual life are especially unendurable to the so-called neurotics among us. These persons manufacture substitute-gratifications for themselves in their symptoms, which, however, are either painful in themselves or become the cause of suffering owing to the difficulties they create with the person's environment and society at large. It is easy to understand the latter fact, but the former presents us with a new problem. But culture demands other sacrifices besides that of sexual gratifications.

We have regarded the difficulties in the development of civilization as part of the general difficulty accompanying all evolution, for we have traced them to the inertia of libido, its disinclination to relinquish an old position in favour of a new one. It is much the same thing if we say that the conflict between civilization and sexuality is caused by the circumstance that sexual love is a relationship between two people, in which a third can only be superfluous or disturbing, whereas civilization is founded on relations between larger groups of persons. When a love-relationship is at its height no room is left for any interest in the surrounding world ; the pair of lovers are sufficient unto themselves, do not even need the child they have in common to make them happy. In no other case does Eros so plainly betray the core of his being, his aim of making one out of many; but when he has achieved it in the proverbial way through the love of two human beings, he is not willing to go further.

From all this we might well imagine that a civilized community could consist of pairs of individuals such as this, libidinally satisfied in each other, and linked to all the others by work and common interests. If this were so, culture would not need to levy energy from sexuality. But such a desirable state of things does not exist and never has existed ; in actuality culture is not content with such limited ties as these ; we see that it endeavours to bind the members of the community to one another by libidinal ties as well, that it makes use of every means and favours every avenue by which powerful identifications can be created among them, and that it exacts a heavy toll of aim-inhibited libido in order to strengthen communities by bonds of friendship between the members.

Restrictions upon sexual life are unavoidable if this object is to be attained. But we cannot see the necessity that forces culture along this path and gives rise to its antagonism to sexuality. It must be due to some disturbing influence not yet detected by us.

We may find the clue in one of the so-called ideal standards of civilized society. It runs: ' Thou shalt love thy neighbour as thyself '. It is world-renowned, undoubtedly older than Christianity which parades it as its proudest profession, yet certainly not very old ; in historical times men still knew nothing of it. We will adopt a naïve attitude towards it, as if we were meeting it for the first time. Thereupon we find ourselves unable to suppress a feeling of astonishment, as at something unnatural. Why should we do this ? What good is it to us ? Above all, how can we do such a thing ? How could it possibly be done ? My love seems to me a valuable thing that I have no right to throw away without reflection. It imposes obligations on me which I must be prepared to make sacrifices to fulfil. If I love someone, he must be worthy of it in some way or other. (I am leaving out of account now the use he may be to me, as well as his possible significance to me as a sexual object ; neither of these two kinds of relationship between us come

F

into question where the injunction to love my neighbour is concerned.) He will be worthy of it if he is so like me in important respects that I can love myself in him ; worthy of it if he is so much more perfect than I that I can love my ideal of myself in him ; I must love him if he is the son of my friend, since the pain my friend would feel if anything untoward happened to him would be my pain—I should have to share it. But if he is a stranger to me and cannot attract me by any value he has in himself or any significance he may have already acquired in my emotional life, it will be hard for me to love him. I shall even be doing wrong if I do, for my love is valued as a privilege by all those belonging to me ; it is an injustice to them if I put a stranger on a level with them. But if I am to love him (with that kind of universal love) simply because he, too, is a denizen of the earth, like an insect or an earthworm or a grass-snake, then I fear that but a small modicum of love will fall to his lot and it would be impossible for me to give him as much as by all the laws of reason I am entitled to retain for myself. What is the point of an injunction promulgated with such solemnity, if reason does not recommend it to us ?

When I look more closely I find still further

difficulties. Not merely is this stranger on the whole not worthy of love, but, to be honest, I must confess he has more claim to my hostility, even to my hatred. He does not seem to have the least trace of love for me, does not show me the slightest consideration. If it will do him any good, he has no hesitation in injuring me, never even asking himself whether the amount of advantage he gains by it bears any proportion to the amount of wrong done to me. What is more, he does not even need to get an advantage from it ; if he can merely get a little pleasure out of it, he thinks nothing of jeering at me, insulting me, slandering me, showing his power over me ; and the more secure he feels himself, or the more helpless I am, with so much more certainty can I expect this behaviour from him towards me. If he behaved differently, if he showed me consideration and did not molest me, I should in any case, without the aforesaid commandment, be willing to treat him similarly. If the high-sounding ordinance had run : ' Love thy neighbour as thy neighbour loves thee ', I should not take objection to it. And there is a second commandment that seems to me even more incomprehensible, and arouses still stronger opposition in me. It is : ' Love thine enemies '. When I think it over, however, I am wrong in treating it as a greater imposition.   It is at bottom the same thing.[1]

I imagine now I hear a voice gravely adjuring me : ' Just because thy neighbour is not worthy of thy love, is probably full of enmity towards thee, thou shouldst love him as thyself '. I then perceive the case to be like that of *Credo quia absurdum*.

Now it is, of course, very probable that my neighbour, when he is commanded to love me as himself, will answer exactly as I have done and reject me for the same reasons.   I hope he will not have the same objective grounds for doing so, but he will hope so as well.   Even so, there are variations in men's behaviour which ethics, disregarding the fact that they are determined, classifies as ' good ' and ' evil '.   As long as these undeniable variations have not been abolished, conformity to the highest ethical standards constitutes a betrayal of the interests of culture, for it puts a

---

[1] A great poet may permit himself, at least in jest, to give utterance to psychological truths that are heavily censured.   Thus Heine : ' Mine is the most peaceable disposition.   My wishes are a humble dwelling with a thatched roof, but a good bed, good food, milk and butter of the freshest, flowers at my windows, some fine tall trees before my door ; and if the good God wants to make me completely happy, he will grant me the joy of seeing some six or seven of my enemies hanging from these trees.   With my heart full of deep emotion I shall forgive them before they die all the wrong they did me in their lifetime—true, one must forgive one's enemies, but not until they are brought to execution.' (Heine, *Gedanken und Einfälle*.)

direct premium on wickedness. One is irresist-
ibly reminded here of an incident in the French
Chamber when capital punishment was being discussed ; the speech of a member who had passionately supported its abolition was being ap-
plauded with loud acclamation, when suddenly a
voice was heard calling out from the back of the
room, ' *Que messieurs les assassins commencent !* '

The bit of truth behind all this—one so eagerly
denied — is that men are not gentle, friendly
creatures wishing for love, who simply defend
themselves if they are attacked, but that a powerful measure of desire for aggression has to be
reckoned as part of their instinctual endowment.
The result is that their neighbour is to them not
only a possible helper or sexual object, but also a
temptation to them to gratify their aggressiveness on him, to exploit his capacity for work without recompense, to use him sexually without his
consent, to seize his possessions, to humiliate him,
to cause him pain, to torture and to kill him.
Homo homini lupus ; who has the courage to dispute it in the face of all the evidence in his own life
and in history ? This aggressive cruelty usually
lies in wait for some provocation, or else it
steps into the service of some other purpose, the
aim of which might as well have been achieved by

milder measures. In circumstances that favour it, when those forces in the mind which ordinarily inhibit it cease to operate, it also manifests itself spontaneously and reveals men as savage beasts to whom the thought of sparing their own kind is alien. Anyone who calls to mind the atrocities of the early migrations, of the invasion by the Huns or by the so-called Mongols under Jenghiz Khan and Tamurlane, of the sack of Jerusalem by the pious Crusaders, even indeed the horrors of the last world-war, will have to bow his head humbly before the truth of this view of man.

The existence of this tendency to aggression which we can detect in ourselves and rightly presume to be present in others is the factor that disturbs our relations with our neighbours and makes it necessary for culture to institute its high demands. Civilized society is perpetually menaced with disintegration through this primary hostility of men towards one another. Their interests in their common work would not hold them together ; the passions of instinct are stronger than reasoned interests. Culture has to call up every possible reinforcement in order to erect barriers against the aggressive instincts of men and hold their manifestations in check by reaction-formations in men's minds. Hence its system of methods by which mankind is to be driven to identifications and aim-inhibited love-relationships ; hence the restrictions on sexual life ; and hence, too, its ideal command to love one's neighbour as oneself, which is really justified by the fact that nothing is so completely at variance with original human nature as this. With all its striving, this endeavour of culture's has so far not achieved very much. Civilization expects to prevent the worst atrocities of brutal violence by taking upon itself the right to employ violence against criminals, but the law is not able to lay hands on the more discreet and subtle forms in which human aggressions are expressed. The time comes when every one of us has to abandon the illusory anticipations with which in our youth we regarded our fellow-men, and when we realize how much hardship and suffering we have been caused in life through their ill-will. It would be unfair, however, to reproach culture with trying to eliminate all disputes and competition from human concerns. These things are undoubtedly indispensable ; but opposition is not necessarily enmity, only it may be misused to make an opening for it.

The Communists believe they have found a way of delivering us from this evil. Man is wholeheartedly good and friendly to his neighbour, they

say, but the system of private property has cor-
rupted his nature. The possession of private
property gives power to the individual and thence
the temptation arises to ill-treat his neighbour ;
the man who is excluded from the possession of
property is obliged to rebel in hostility against the
oppressor.   If private property were abolished, all
valuables held in common and all allowed to share
in the enjoyment of them, ill-will and enmity
would disappear from among men.   Since all
needs would be satisfied, none would have any
reason to regard another as an enemy ; all would
willingly undertake the work which is necessary.
I have no concern with any economic criticisms of
the communistic system ; I cannot enquire into
whether the abolition of private property is advantageous and expedient.[1]   But I am able to
recognize that psychologically it is founded on an
untenable illusion.   By abolishing private property one deprives the human love of aggression

[1] Anyone who has been through the misery of poverty in his
youth, and has endured the indifference and arrogance of those
who have possessions, should be exempt from the suspicion that
he has no understanding of or goodwill towards the endeavours
made to fight the economic inequality of men and all that it
leads to. To be sure, if an attempt is made to base this fight upon
an abstract demand for equality for all in the name of justice,
there is a very obvious objection to be made, namely, that nature
began the injustice by the highly unequal way in which she
endows individuals physically and mentally, for which there is
no help.

of one of its instruments, a strong one undoubtedly, but assuredly not the strongest. It in no way alters the individual differences in power and influence which are turned by aggressiveness to its own use, nor does it change the nature of the instinct in any way. This instinct did not arise as the result of property; it reigned almost supreme in primitive times when possessions were still extremely scanty; it shows itself already in the nursery when possessions have hardly grown out of their original anal shape; it is at the bottom of all the relations of affection and love between human beings—possibly with the single exception of that of a mother to her male child. Suppose that personal rights to material goods are done away with, there still remain prerogatives in sexual relationships, which must arouse the strongest rancour and most violent enmity among men and women who are otherwise equal. Let us suppose this were also to be removed by instituting complete liberty in sexual life, so that the family, the germ-cell of culture, ceased to exist; one could not, it is true, foresee the new paths on which cultural development might then proceed, but one thing one would be bound to expect and that is that the ineffaceable feature of human nature would follow wherever it led.

Men clearly do not find it easy to do without satisfaction of this tendency to aggression that is in them ; when deprived of satisfaction of it they are ill at ease.　There is an advantage, not to be undervalued, in the existence of smaller communities, through which the aggressive instinct can find an outlet in enmity towards those outside the group.　It is always possible to unite considerable numbers of men in love towards one another, so long as there are still some remaining as objects for aggressive manifestations.　I once interested myself in the peculiar fact that peoples whose territories are adjacent, and are otherwise closely related, are always at feud with and ridiculing each other, as, for instance, the Spaniards and the Portuguese, the North and South Germans, the English and the Scotch, and so on.　I gave it the name of ' narcissism in respect of minor differences ', which does not do much to explain it.　One can now see that it is a convenient and relatively harmless form of satisfaction for aggressive tendencies, through which cohesion amongst the members of a group is made easier.　The Jewish people, scattered in all directions as they are, have in this way rendered services which deserve recognition to the development of culture in the countries where they settled ; but unfortunately not all the massacres of Jews in the Middle Ages sufficed to procure peace and security for their Christian contemporaries. Once the apostle Paul had laid down universal love between all men as the foundation of his Christian community, the inevitable consequence in Christianity was the utmost intolerance towards all who remained outside of it ; the Romans, who had not founded their state on love, were not given to lack of religious toleration, although religion was a concern of the state and the state was permeated through and through with it. Neither was it an unaccountable chance that the dream of a German world-dominion evoked a complementary movement towards anti-semitism ; and it is quite intelligible that the attempt to establish a new communistic type of culture in Russia should find psychological support in the persecution of the bourgeois. One only wonders, with some concern, however, how the Soviets will manage when they have exterminated their bourgeois entirely.

If civilization requires such sacrifices, not only of sexuality but also of the aggressive tendencies in mankind, we can better understand why it should be so hard for men to feel happy in it. In actual fact primitive man was better off in this respect, for he knew nothing of any restrictions on his instincts.

As a set-off against this, his prospects of enjoying his happiness for any length of time were very slight.   Civilized man has exchanged some part of his chances of happiness for a measure of security. We will not forget, however, that in the primal family only the head of it enjoyed this instinctual freedom ;   the other members lived in slavish thraldom.   The antithesis between a minority enjoying cultural advantages and a majority who are robbed of them was therefore most extreme in that primeval period of culture.   With regard to the primitive human types living at the present time, careful investigation has revealed that their instinctual life is by no means to be envied on account of its freedom ; it is subject to restrictions of a different kind but perhaps even more rigorous than is that of modern civilized man.

In rightly finding fault, as we thus do, with our present state of civilization for so inadequately providing us with what we require to make us happy in life, and for the amount of suffering of a probably avoidable nature it lays us open to—in doing our utmost to lay bare the roots of its deficiencies by our unsparing criticisms, we are undoubtedly exercising our just rights and not showing ourselves enemies of culture.   We may expect that in the course of time changes will be carried out in our civilization so that it becomes more satisfying to our needs and no longer open to the reproaches we have made against it. But perhaps we shall also accustom ourselves to the idea that there are certain difficulties inherent in the very nature of culture which will not yield to any efforts at reform. Over and above the obligations of putting restrictions upon our instincts, which we see to be inevitable, we are imminently threatened with the dangers of a state one may call '*la misère psychologique*' of groups. This danger is most menacing where the social forces of cohesion consist predominantly of identifications of the individuals in the group with one another, whilst leading personalities fail to acquire the significance that should fall to them in the process of group-formation.[1] The state of civilization in America at the present day offers a good opportunity for studying this injurious effect of civilization which we have reason to dread. But I will resist the temptation to enter upon a criticism of American culture ; I have no desire to give the impression that I would employ American methods myself.

[1] Cf. *Group Psychology and the Analysis of the Ego* (1921). London : Hogarth Press, 1922.

VI

NEVER before in any of my previous writings have I had the feeling so strongly as I have now that what I am describing is common knowledge, that I am requisitioning paper and ink, and in due course the labour of compositors and printers, in order to expound things that in themselves are obvious. For this reason, if it should appear that the recognition of a special independent instinct of aggression would entail a modification of the psycho-analytical theory of instincts, I should be glad enough to seize upon the idea.

We shall see that this is not so, that it is merely a matter of coming to closer quarters with a conclusion to which we long ago committed ourselves and following it out to its logical consequences. The whole of analytic theory has evolved gradually enough, but the theory of instincts has groped its way forward under greater difficulties than any other part of it. And yet a theory of instincts was so indispensable for the rest that something had to be adopted in place of it. In my utter perplexity at the beginning, I took as my starting-point the poet-philosopher Schiller's aphorism, that hunger and love make the world go round.   Hunger would serve to represent those instincts which aim at preservation of the individual ; love seeks for objects : its chief function, which is favoured in every way by nature, is preservation of the species. Thus first arose the contrast between ego instincts and object instincts.   For the energy of the latter instincts and exclusively for them I introduced the term libido ; an antithesis was thus formed between the ego instincts and the libidinal instincts directed towards objects, *i.e.* love in its widest sense.   One of these object instincts, the sadistic, certainly stood out from the rest in that its aim was so very unloving ; moreover, it clearly allied itself in many of its aspects with the ego instincts, and its close kinship with instincts of mastery without any libidinal purpose could not be concealed, but these ambiguities could be overcome ; in spite of them, sadism plainly belonged to sexual life—the game of cruelty could take the place of the game of love. Neurosis appeared as the outcome of a struggle between the interests of self-preservation and the claims of libido, a struggle in which the ego was victorious, but at the price of great suffering and renunciations.

Every analyst will admit that none of this even now reads like a statement long since recognized as erroneous. All the same, modifications had to be made as our researches advanced from the repressed to the repressing, from the object instincts to the ego. A cardinal point in this advance was the introduction of the concept of narcissism, *i.e.* the idea that libido cathects the ego itself, that its first dwelling-place was in the ego, and that the latter remains to some extent its permanent headquarters. This narcissistic libido turns in the direction of objects, thus becoming object-libido, and can transform itself back into narcissistic libido. The concept of narcissism made it possible to consider the traumatic neuroses, as well as many diseases bordering on the psychoses, and also the latter themselves, from the psycho-analytic angle. It was not necessary to abandon the view that the transference-neuroses are attempts on the part of the ego to guard itself against sexuality, but the concept of the libido was jeopardized. Since the ego-instincts were found to be libidinal as well, it seemed for a time inevitable that libido should become synonymous with instinctual energy in general, as C. G. Jung had previously advocated. Yet there still remained in me a kind of conviction, for which as yet there were no grounds, that the instincts could not all be of the same nature. I made the next step in *Beyond the Pleasure Principle* (1920), when the repetition-compulsion and the conservative character of instinctual life first struck me. On the basis of speculations concerning the origin of life and of biological parallels, I drew the conclusion that, beside the instinct preserving the organic substance and binding it into ever larger units,[1] there must exist another in antithesis to this, which would seek to dissolve these units and reinstate their antecedent inorganic state. That is to say, a death instinct as well as Eros ; the phenomena of life would then be explicable from the interplay of the two and their counteracting effects on each other. It was not easy, however, to demonstrate the working of this hypothetical death instinct. The manifestations of Eros were conspicuous and audible enough ; one might assume that the death instinct worked silently within the organism towards its disintegration, but that, of course, was no proof. The idea that part of the instinct became directed towards the outer world and then showed itself as an instinct of aggression and destruction carried us a step further. The

[1] The contradiction between the tireless tendency of Eros to spread ever further and the general conservative nature of the instincts here becomes very noticeable ; it would serve as the starting-point of enquiries into further problems.

G

instinct would thus itself have been pressed into the service of Eros, in that the organism would be destroying something animate or inanimate outside itself instead of itself. Conversely, any cessation of this flow outwards must have the effect of intensifying the self-destruction which in any case would always be going on within. From this example one could then surmise that the two kinds of instincts seldom—perhaps never—appear in isolation, but always mingle with each other in different, very varying proportions, and so make themselves unrecognizable to us. Sadism, long since known to us as a component-instinct of sexuality, would represent a particularly strong admixture of the instinct of destruction into the love impulse ; while its counterpart, masochism, would be an alliance between sexuality and the destruction at work within the self, in consequence of which the otherwise imperceptible destructive trend became directly evident and palpable.

The assumption of the existence of a death instinct or a destruction instinct has roused opposition even in analytical circles ; I know that there is a great tendency to ascribe all that is dangerous and hostile in love rather to a fundamental bipolarity in its own nature. The conceptions I have summarized here I first put forward only tentatively, but in the course of time they have won such a hold over me that I can no longer think in any other way. To my mind they are theoretically far more fruitful than any others it is possible to employ ; they provide us with that simplification, without either ignoring or doing violence to the facts, which is what we strive after in scientific work.   I know that we have always had before our eyes manifestations of the destruction instinct fused with erotism, directed outwards and inwards in sadism and masochism ; but I can no longer understand how we could have overlooked the universality of non-erotic aggression and destruction, and could have omitted to give it its due significance in our inter-pretation of life.   (It is true that the destructive trend that is directed inwards, when it is not erotically tinged, usually eludes our perceptions.) I can remember my own defensive attitude when the idea of an instinct of destruction first made its appearance in psycho-analytical literature and how long it took until I became accessible to it.   That others should have shown the same resistance, and still show it, surprises me less.   Those who love fairy-tales do not like it when people speak of the innate tendencies in mankind towards aggression, destruc-tion and, in addition, cruelty.   For God has made them in his own image, with his own perfections ;

no one wants to be reminded how hard it is to re-
concile the undeniable existence—in spite of all the
protestations of Christian Science—of evil with His
omnipotence and supreme goodness. The devil is, in
fact, the best way out in acquittal of God ; he can
be used to play the same economic rôle of outlet as
Jews in the world of Aryan ideals.   But even so,
one can just as well hold God responsible for the
existence of the devil as for the evil he personifies.
In view of these difficulties, it is expedient for every
man to make humble obeisance on suitable occasions in honour of the high-minded nature of men ;
it will assist him to become universally beloved and
much shall be forgiven unto him on account of it.[1]

[1] In Goethe's Mephistopheles we have a quite exceptionally
striking identification of the principle of evil with the instinct of
destruction :

> ' All entities that be
> Deserve their end—nonentity.'

>   .   .   .   .   .

> ' So all that you name sin, destruction—
> Wickedness, briefly—proves to be
> The native element for me.'

As his adversary, the devil himself cites not what is holy and
good, but the power in nature working towards the creation and
renewal of life—that is, Eros.

> ' From air, from water, germs in thousands,
> As from the soil, break forth, break free,
> Dry, wet, warm, cold—a pullulation !
> Had I not laid on flame a reservation,
> Nothing were set apart for me.'

The name libido can again be used to denote the manifestations of the power of Eros in contradistinction to the energy of the death instinct.[1] We must confess that it is more difficult for us to detect the latter, and to a great extent we can merely conjecture its existence as a background to Eros, also that it eludes us wherever it is not betrayed by a fusion with Eros. In sadism, where it bends the erotic aim to its own will and yet at the same time gratifies the sexual craving completely, we can obtain the clearest insight into its nature and its relation to Eros. But even where it shows itself without any sexual purpose, even in the blindest frenzy of destructiveness, one cannot ignore the fact that satisfaction of it is accompanied by an extraordinarily intense narcissistic enjoyment, due to the fulfilment it brings to the ego of its oldest omnipotence-wishes. The instinct of destruction, when tempered and harnessed (as it were, inhibited in its aim) and directed towards objects, is compelled to provide the ego with satisfaction of its needs and with power over nature. Since the assumption of its existence is based essentially on theoretical grounds, it must be confessed that it is not entirely proof against theoretical

[1] Our present point of view can be roughly expressed in the statement that libido participates in every instinctual manifestation, but that not everything in that manifestation is libido.

objections.   But this is how things appear to us
now in the present state of our knowledge ; future
research and reflection will undoubtedly bring
further light which will decide the question.

In all that follows I take up the standpoint that
the tendency to aggression is an innate, independent, instinctual disposition in man, and I
come back now to the statement that it constitutes
the most powerful obstacle to culture.   At one
point in the course of this discussion the idea took
possession of us that culture was a peculiar process
passing over human life and we are still under the
influence of this idea.   We may add to this that
the process proves to be in the service of Eros,
which aims at binding together single human individuals, then families, then tribes, races, nations,
into one great unity, that of humanity.   Why this
has to be done we do not know ; it is simply the
work of Eros.   These masses of men must be bound
to one another libidinally ; necessity alone, the
advantages of common work, would not hold them
together.   The natural instinct of aggressiveness in
man, the hostility of each one against all and of
all against each one, opposes this programme of
civilization.   This instinct of aggression is the
derivative and main representative of the death
instinct we have found alongside of Eros, sharing

his rule over the earth.   And now, it seems to me, the meaning of the evolution of culture is no longer a riddle to us.   It must present to us the struggle between Eros and Death, between the instincts of life and the instincts of destruction, as it works itself out in the human species.   This struggle is what all life essentially consists of and so the evolution of civilization may be simply described as the struggle of the human species for existence.[1] And it is this battle of the Titans that our nurses and governesses try to compose with their lullaby-song of Heaven !

[1] And we may probably add more precisely that its form was necessarily determined after some definite event which still remains to be discovered.

VII

WHY do the animals, kin to ourselves, not manifest any such cultural struggle? Oh, we don't know. Very probably certain of them, bees, ants, termites, had to strive for thousands of centuries before they found the way to those state institutions, that division of functions, those restrictions upon individuals, which we admire them for to-day. It is characteristic of our present state that we know by our own feelings that we should not think ourselves happy in any of these communities of the animal world, or in any of the rôles they delegate to individuals. With other animal species it may be that a temporary deadlock has been reached between the influences of their environment and the instincts contending within them, so that a cessation of development has taken place. In primitive man a fresh access of libido may have kindled a new spurt of energy on the part of the instinct of destruction. There are a great many questions in all this to which as yet we have no answer.

Another question concerns us more closely now. What means does civilization make use of to hold in check the aggressiveness that opposes it, to make it harmless, perhaps to get rid of it ? Some of these measures we have already come to know, though not yet the one that is apparently the most important. We can study it in the evolution of the individual. What happens in him to render his craving for aggression innocuous ? Something very curious, that we should never have guessed and that yet seems simple enough. The aggressiveness is introjected, 'internalized'; in fact, it is sent back where it came from, *i.e.* directed against the ego. It is there taken over by a part of the ego that distinguishes itself from the rest as a super-ego, and now, in the form of 'conscience', exercises the same propensity to harsh aggressiveness against the ego that the ego would have liked to enjoy against others. The tension between the strict super-ego and the subordinate ego we call the sense of guilt; it manifests itself as the need for punishment. Civilization therefore obtains the mastery over the dangerous love of aggression in individuals by enfeebling and disarming it and setting up an institution within their minds to keep watch over it, like a garrison in a conquered city.

As to the origin of the sense of guilt, analysts

have different views from those of the psychologists; nor is it easy for analysts to explain it either.   First of all, when one asks how a sense of guilt arises in anyone, one is told something one cannot dispute : people feel guilty (pious people call it ' sinful ') when they have done something they know to be ' bad '.   But then one sees how little this answer tells one.   Perhaps after some hesitation one will add that a person who has not actually committed a bad act, but has merely become aware of the intention to do so, can also hold himself guilty ; and then one will ask why in this case the intention is counted as equivalent to the deed.   In both cases, however, one is presupposing that wickedness has already been recognized as reprehensible, as something that ought not to be put into execution. How is this judgement arrived at ?   One may reject the suggestion of an original—as one might say, natural—capacity for discriminating between good and evil.   Evil is often not at all that which would injure or endanger the ego ; on the contrary, it can also be something that it desires, that would give it pleasure.   An extraneous influence is evidently at work ; it is this that decides what is to be called good and bad.   Since their own feelings would not have led men along the same path, they must have had a motive for obeying this extraneous influence.

It is easy to discover this motive in man's helplessness and dependence upon others ; it can best be designated the dread of losing love.   If he loses the love of others on whom he is dependent, he will forfeit also their protection against many dangers, and above all he runs the risk that this stronger person will show his superiority in the form of punishing him.   What is bad is, therefore, to begin with, whatever causes one to be threatened with a loss of love ; because of the dread of this loss, one must desist from it.   That is why it makes little difference whether one has already committed the bad deed or only intends to do so ; in either case the danger begins only when the authority has found it out, and the latter would behave in the same way in both cases.

We call this state of mind a ' bad conscience ' but actually it does not deserve this name, for at this stage the sense of guilt is obviously only the dread of losing love, ' social ' anxiety.   In a little child it can never be anything else, but in many adults too it has only changed in so far as the larger human community takes the place of the father or of both parents.   Consequently such people habitually permit themselves to do any bad deed that procures them something they want, if only they are sure that no authority will discover it or make them suffer for it ; their anxiety relates only to the possibility of detection.[1] Present-day society has to take into account the prevalence of this state of mind.

A great change takes place· as soon as the authority has been internalized by the development of a super-ego. The manifestations of conscience are then raised to a new level ; to be accurate, one should not call them conscience and sense of guilt before this.[2] At this point the dread of discovery ceases to operate and also once for all any difference between doing evil and wishing to do it, since nothing is hidden from the super-ego, not even thoughts. The real seriousness of the situation has vanished, it is true : for the new authority, the super-ego, has no motive, as far as we know, for ill-treating the ego with which it is itself closely bound up. But the influence of the genetic derivation of these things, which causes what has been outlived and surmounted to be re-lived, manifests itself so that on the whole things remain as they were at the beginning. The super-ego torments the sinful ego with the same feelings of dread and watches for opportunities whereby the outer world can be made to punish it.

[1] One is reminded of Rousseau's famous mandarin !

[2] Every reasonable person will understand and take into account that in this descriptive survey things that in reality occur

At this second stage of development, conscience exhibits a peculiarity which was absent in the first and is not very easy to account for. That is, the more righteous a man is the stricter and more suspicious will his conscience be, so that ultimately it is precisely those people who have carried holiness farthest who reproach themselves with the deepest sinfulness. This means that virtue forfeits some of her promised reward ; the submissive and abstemious ego does not enjoy the trust and confidence of its mentor, and, as it seems, strives in vain to earn it. Now, to this some people will be ready to object that these difficulties are artificialities. A relatively strict and vigilant conscience is the very sign of a virtuous man, and though saints may proclaim themselves sinners, they are not so wrong, in view of the temptations of instinctual gratifications to which they are peculiarly liable—since, as we know, temptations do but increase under constant privation, whereas they subside, at any rate temporarily, if they are sometimes gratified. The field of ethics is rich in problems, and another of the facts we find here is

by gradual transitions are sharply differentiated and that the mere existence of a super-ego is not the only factor concerned, but also its relative strength and sphere of influence. All that has been said above in regard to conscience and guilt, moreover, is common knowledge and practically undisputed.

that misfortune, *i.e.* external deprivation, greatly intensifies the strength of conscience in the super-ego. As long as things go well with a man, his conscience is lenient and lets the ego do all kinds of things; when some calamity befalls, he holds an inquisition within, discovers his sin, heightens the standards of his conscience, imposes abstinences on himself and punishes himself with penances.[1] Whole peoples have acted in this way and still do so. But this is easily explained from the original infantile stage of conscience which, as we thus see, is not abandoned after the introjection into the super-ego, but persists alongside and behind the latter. Fate is felt to be a substitute for the agency of the parents: adversity means that one is no longer loved by this highest power of all, and, threatened by this loss of love, one humbles one-self again before the representative of the parents in the super-ego which in happier days one had tried to disregard. This becomes especially clear when destiny is looked upon in the strictly religious sense as the expression of God's will and

---

[1] This increased sensitivity of morals in consequence of ill-luck has been illustrated by Mark Twain in a delicious little story: *The First Melon I ever Stole*. This melon, as it happened, was unripe. I heard Mark Twain tell the story himself in one of his lectures. After he had given out the title, he stopped and asked himself in a doubtful way: ' Was it the first ? ' This was the whole story.

nothing else. The people of Israel believed themselves to be God's favourite child, and when the great Father hurled visitation after visitation upon them, it still never shook them in this belief or caused them to doubt His power and His justice; they proceeded instead to bring their prophets into the world to declare their sinfulness to them and out of their sense of guilt they constructed the stringent commandments of their priestly religion. It is curious how differently a savage behaves! If he has had bad fortune, he does not throw the blame on himself, but on his fetish, who has plainly not done his duty by him, and he belabours it instead of punishing himself.

Hence we know of two sources for feelings of guilt : that arising from the dread of authority and the later one from the dread of the super-ego. The first one compels us to renounce instinctual gratification ; the other presses over and above this towards punishment, since the persistence of forbidden wishes cannot be concealed from the super-ego. We have also heard how the severity of the super-ego, the rigour of conscience, is to be explained. It simply carries on the severity of external authority which it has succeeded and to some extent replaced. We see now how renunciation of instinctual gratification is related to the sense of guilt. Originally, it is true, renunciation is the consequence of a dread of external authority ; one gives up pleasures so as not to lose its love. Having made this renunciation, one is quits with authority, so to speak ; no feeling of guilt should remain. But with the dread of the super-ego the case is different. Renunciation of gratification does not suffice here, for the wish persists and is not capable of being hidden from the super-ego. In spite of the renunciations made, feelings of guilt will be experienced and this is a great disadvantage economically of the erection of the super-ego, or, as one may say, of the formation of conscience. Renunciation no longer has a completely absolving effect ; virtuous restraint is no longer rewarded by the assurance of love ; a threatened external unhappiness—loss of love and punishment meted out by external authority—has been exchanged for a lasting inner unhappiness, the tension of a sense of guilt.

These inter-relations are so complicated and at the same time so important that, in spite of the dangers of repetition, I will consider them again from another angle. The chronological sequence would thus be as follows: first, instinct-renunciation due to dread of an aggression by external authority—this is, of course, tantamount to the dread of loss of love, for love is a protection against these punitive aggressions. Then follows the erection of an internal authority, and instinctual renunciation due to dread of it—that is, dread of conscience. In the second case, there is the equivalence of wicked acts and wicked intentions ; hence comes the sense of guilt, the need for punishment. The aggressiveness of conscience carries on the aggressiveness of authority. Thus far all seems to be clear ; but how can we find a place in this scheme for the effect produced by misfortune (*i.e.* renunciations externally imposed), for the effect it has of increasing the rigour of conscience ? how account for the exceptional stringency of conscience in the best men, those least given to rebel against it ? We have already explained both these peculiarities of conscience, but probably we still have an impression that these explanations do not go to the root of the matter, and that they leave something still unexplained. And here at last comes in an idea which is quite peculiar to psycho-analysis and alien to ordinary ways of thinking. Its nature enables us to understand why the whole matter necessarily seemed so confused and obscure to us. It tells us this : in the beginning conscience (more correctly, the anxiety which later became conscience) was the

H

cause of instinctual renunciation, but later this relation is reversed. Every renunciation then becomes a dynamic fount of conscience ; every fresh abandonment of gratification increases its severity and intolerance ; and if we could only bring it better into harmony with what we already know about the development of conscience, we should be tempted to make the following paradoxical statement : Conscience is the result of instinctual renunciation, or : Renunciation (externally imposed) gives rise to conscience, which then demands further renunciations.

The contradiction between this proposition and our previous knowledge about the genesis of conscience is not in actual fact so very great and we can see a way in which it may be still further reduced. In order to state the problem more easily, let us select the example of the instinct of aggression, and let us suppose that the renunciation in question is always a renunciation of aggression. This is, of course, merely a provisional assumption. The effect of instinctual renunciation on conscience then operates as follows : every impulse of aggression which we omit to gratify is taken over by the super-ego and goes to heighten its aggressiveness (against the ego). It does not fit in well with this that the original aggressiveness of con-

science should represent a continuance of the
rigour of external authority, and so have nothing
to do with renunciation. But we can get rid of
this discrepancy if we presume a different origin
for the first quantum of aggressiveness with which
the super-ego was endowed. When authority prevented the child from enjoying the first but most
important gratifications of all, aggressive impulses of considerable intensity must have been
evoked in it, irrespective of the particular nature
of the instinctual deprivations concerned. The
child must necessarily have had to give up the
satisfaction of these revengeful aggressive wishes.
In this situation, in which it is economically so
hard pressed, it has recourse to certain mechan-
isms well known to us ; by the process of identification it absorbs into itself the invulnerable authority,
which then becomes the super-ego and comes into
possession of all the aggressiveness which the
child would gladly have exercised against it. The
child's ego has to content itself with the unhappy
rôle of the authority—the father—who has been
thus degraded. It is, as so often, a reversal of the
original situation, ' If I were father and you my
child, I would treat *you* badly '. The relation
between super-ego and ego is a reproduction, distorted by a wish, of the real relations between the

ego, before it was subdivided, and an external object. That is also typical. The essential difference, however, is that the original severity of the super-ego does not—or not so much—represent the severity which has been experienced or anticipated from the object, but expresses the child's own aggressiveness towards the latter. If this is correct, one could truly assert that conscience is formed in the beginning from the suppression of an aggressive impulse and strengthened as time goes on by each fresh suppression of the kind.

Now, which of these two theories is the true one ? The earlier, which seemed genetically so unassailable, or the new one, which rounds off our theories in such a welcome manner ? Clearly, they are both justified, and by the evidence, too, of direct observation ; they do not contradict each other, and even coincide at one point, for the child's revengeful aggressiveness will be in part provoked by the amount of punishing aggression that it anticipates from the father. Experience has shown, however, that the severity which a child's super-ego develops in no way corresponds to the severity of the treatment it has itself experienced.[1] It seems to be independent of the

[1] As has rightly been emphasized by Melanie Klein and other English writers.

latter ; a child which has been very leniently treated can acquire a very strict conscience. But it would also be wrong to exaggerate this independence ; it is not difficult to assure oneself that strict upbringing also has a strong influence on the formation of a child's super-ego. It comes to this, that the formation of the super-ego and the development of conscience are determined in part by innate constitutional factors and in part by the influence of the actual environment ; and that is in no way surprising—on the contrary, it is the invariable aetiological condition of all such processes.[1]

It may also be said that when a child reacts to the first great instinctual deprivations with an excessive aggressiveness and a corresponding strictness of its super-ego, it is thereby following a phylogenetic prototype, unheedful of what reaction would in reality be justified ; for the father of primitive times was certainly terrifying, and one may safely attribute the utmost degree of aggressiveness to him. The differences between the two theories of the genesis of conscience are thus still further diminished if one passes from individual to phylogenetic development. But then, on the other

[1] In his *Psychoanalyse der Gesamtpersönlichkeit*, 1927, Franz Alexander has, in connection with Aichhorn's study of dissocial

hand, we find a new important difference between the two processes.   We cannot disregard the conclusion that man's sense of guilt has its origin in the Oedipus complex and was acquired when the father was killed by the association of the brothers. At that time the aggression was not suppressed but carried out, and it is this same act of aggression whose suppression in the child we regard as the source of feelings of guilt.   Now, I should not be surprised if a reader were to cry out angrily : So it makes no difference whether one does kill one's father or does not, one gets a feeling of guilt in either case !   Here I should think one may be allowed some doubts.   Either it is not true that guilt is evoked by suppressed aggressiveness or else the whole story about the father-murder is a romance, and primeval man did not kill his father any more often than people do nowadays.   Be-

behaviour in children, discussed the two main types of pathogenic methods of training, that of excessive severity and of spoiling. The ' unduly lenient and indulgent ' father fosters the development of an over-strict super-ego because, in face of the love which is showered on it, the child has no other way of disposing of its aggressiveness than to turn it inwards.   In neglected children who grow up without any love the tension between ego and super-ego is lacking ; their aggressions can be directed externally. Apart from any constitutional factor which may be present, therefore, one may say that a strict conscience arises from the co-operation of two factors in the environment : the deprivation of instinctual gratification which evokes the child's aggressiveness, and the love it receives which turns this aggressiveness inwards, where it is taken over by the super-ego.

sides this, if it is not a romance but a plausible piece of history, it would only be an instance of what we all expect to happen, namely, that one feels guilty because one has really done something which cannot be justified. And what we are all waiting for is for psycho-analysis to give us an explanation of this reaction, which at any rate is something that happens every day.'

This is true, and we must make good the omission. There is no great mystery about it either. When one has feelings of guilt after one has committed some crime and because of it, this feeling should more properly be called *remorse*. It relates only to the one act, and clearly it presupposes that *conscience*, the capacity for feelings of guilt, was already in existence before the deed. Remorse of this kind can, therefore, never help us to find out the source of conscience and feelings of guilt in general. In these everyday instances the course of events is usually as follows : an instinctual need acquires the strength to achieve fulfilment in spite of conscience, the strength of which also has its limits, whereupon the inevitable reduction of the need after satisfaction restores the earlier balance of forces. Psycho-analysis is quite justified, therefore, in excluding the case of a sense of guilt through remorse from this discussion, however frequently it may occur and however great its importance may be practically.

But if man's sense of guilt goes back to the murder of the father, that was undoubtedly an instance of 'remorse', and yet are we to suppose that there were no conscience and feelings of guilt before the act on that occasion ? If so, where did the remorse come from then ? This instance must explain to us the riddle of the sense of guilt and so make an end of our difficulties. And it will do so, as I believe. This remorse was the result of the very earliest primal ambivalence of feelings towards the father : the sons hated him, but they loved him too ; after their hate against him had been satisfied by their aggressive acts, their love came to expression in their remorse about the deed, set up the super-ego by identification with the father, gave it the father's power to punish as he would have done the aggression they had performed, and created the restrictions which should prevent a repetition of the deed. And since impulses to aggressions against the father were repeated in the next generations, the feelings of guilt, too, persisted, and were further reinforced every time an aggression was suppressed anew and made over to the super-ego. At this point, it seems to me, we can at last clearly perceive the part played by love in the origin of conscience and the fatal inevitableness of the sense of guilt. It is not really a decisive matter whether one has killed one's father or abstained from the deed; one must feel guilty in either case, for guilt is the expression of the conflict of ambivalence, the eternal struggle between Eros and the destructive or death instinct. This conflict is engendered as soon as man is confronted with the task of living with his fellows; as long as he knows no other form of life in common but that of the family, it must express itself in the Oedipus complex, cause the development of conscience and create the first feelings of guilt. When mankind tries to institute wider forms of communal life, the same conflict continues to arise—in forms derived from the past—and intensified so that a further reinforcement of the sense of guilt results. Since culture obeys an inner erotic impulse which bids it bind mankind into a closely-knit mass, it can achieve this aim only by means of its vigilance in fomenting an ever-increasing sense of guilt. That which began in relation to the father ends in relation to the community. If civilization is an inevitable course of development from the group of the family to the group of humanity as a whole, then an intensification of the sense of guilt—resulting from the innate conflict of ambivalence, from the eternal struggle between the love and the death trends—will be inextricably bound up with it, until perhaps the sense of guilt may swell to a magnitude that individuals can hardly support. One is reminded of the telling accusation made by the great poet against the ' heavenly forces ' :

> Ye set our feet on this life's road,
> Ye watch our guilty, erring courses,
> Then leave us, bowed beneath our load,
> For earth its every debt enforces.[1]

And one may heave a sigh at the thought that it is vouchsafed to a few, with hardly an effort, to salve from the whirlpool of their own emotions the deepest truths, to which we others have to force our way, ceaselessly groping amid torturing uncertainties.

[1] Goethe, *Wilhelm Meister*. The Song of the Harper.

VIII

ON reaching the end of such a journey as this, the author must beg his readers to pardon him for not having been a more skilful guide, not sparing them bleak stretches of country at times and laborious detours at others. There is no doubt that it could have been done better. I will now try to make some amends.

First of all, I suspect the reader feels that the discussion about the sense of guilt oversteps its proper boundaries in this essay and takes up too much space, so that the rest of the subject-matter, which is not always closely connected with it, gets pushed on one side. This may have spoilt the composition of the work ; but it faithfully corresponds to my intention to represent the sense of guilt as the most important problem in the evolution of culture, and to convey that the price of progress in civilization is paid in forfeiting happiness through the heightening of the sense of guilt.[1]

---

[1] ' Thus conscience does make cowards of us all. . . .

That the upbringing of young people at the present day conceals from them the part sexuality will play in their lives is not

What sounds puzzling in this statement, which is the final conclusion of our whole investigation, is probably due to the quite peculiar relation —as yet completely unexplained—the sense of guilt has to our consciousness. In the common cases of remorse which we think normal it becomes clearly perceptible to consciousness ; indeed, we often speak of ' consciousness of guilt ' instead of sense of guilt. In our study of the neuroses, in which we have found invaluable clues towards an understanding of normal people, we find some very contradictory states of affairs in this respect. In one of these maladies, the obsessional neurosis, the sense of guilt makes itself loudly heard in consciousness ; it dominates the clinical picture as well as the patient's life and lets hardly anything else appear alongside of it. But in most of the other types and forms of neurosis it remains com-

---

the only reproach we are obliged to bring against it. It offends too in not preparing them for the aggressions of which they are destined to become the objects. Sending the young out into life with such a false psychological orientation is as if one were to equip people going on a Polar expedition with summer clothing and maps of the Italian lakes. One can clearly see that ethical standards are being misused in a way. The strictness of these standards would not do much harm if education were to say : ' This is how men ought to be in order to be happy and make others happy, but you have to reckon with their not being so.' Instead of this the young are made to believe that everyone else conforms to the standard of ethics, *i.e.* that everyone else is good. And then on this is based the demand that the young shall be so too.

pletely unconscious, without its effect being any
less great, however.   Our patients do not believe
us when we ascribe an ' unconscious sense of guilt
to them ; in order to become even moderately intelligible to them we have to explain that the sense
of guilt expresses itself in an unconscious seeking
for punishment.   But its connection with the
form of the neurosis is not to be over-estimated ;
even in the obsessional neurosis there are people
who are not aware of their sense of guilt or who
perceive it only as a tormenting uneasiness or kind
of anxiety and then not until they are prevented
from carrying out certain actions.   We ought some
day to be able at last to understand these things ;
as yet we cannot.   Here perhaps is the place to
remark that at bottom the sense of guilt is nothing
but a topographical variety of anxiety, and that
in its later phases it coincides completely with the
dread of the super-ego.   The relation of anxiety
to consciousness, moreover, is characterized by
the same extraordinary variations.   Somewhere or
other there is always anxiety hidden behind all
symptoms ; at one moment, however, it sweeps
into consciousness, drowning everything else with
its clamour, and at the next it secretes itself so
completely that we are forced to speak of unconscious anxiety—or if we want to have a cleaner

conscience psychologically, since anxiety is after all only a perception—of possibilities of anxiety. Consequently it is very likely that the sense of guilt produced by culture is not perceived as such and remains to a great extent unconscious, or comes to expression as a sort of uneasiness or discontent for which other motivations are sought. The different religions at any rate have never overlooked the part played by the sense of guilt in civilization. What is more, they come forward with a claim, which I have not considered elsewhere,[1] to save mankind from this sense of guilt, which they call sin. We indeed have drawn our conclusions, from the way in which in Christianity this salvation is won—the sacrificial death of one who therewith takes the whole of the common guilt of all upon himself—about the occasion on which this primal sense of guilt was first acquired, that is, the occasion which was also the inception of culture.[2]

It will not be very important, but it may be just as well to go more precisely into the meaning of certain words like super-ego, conscience, sense of guilt, need for punishment, remorse, which we have perhaps often used too loosely and in place of one another. They all relate to the same situation,

[1] I mean in *The Future of an Illusion.*
[2] *Totem und Tabu* (1912).

but they denote different aspects of it.   The super-ego is an agency or institution in the mind whose existence we have inferred : conscience is a function we ascribe, among others, to the super-ego ; it consists of watching over and judging the actions and intentions of the ego, exercising the functions of a censor.   The sense of guilt, the severity of the super-ego, is therefore the same thing as the rigour of conscience ; it is the perception the ego has that it is watched in this way, the ego's appreciation of the tension between its strivings and the standards of the super-ego ; and the anxiety that lies behind all these relations, the dread of that critical institution, the need for punishment, is an instinctual manifestation on the part of the ego, which has become masochistic under the influence of the sadistic super-ego, *i.e.* which has brought a part of the instinct of destruction at work within itself into the service of an erotic attachment to the super-ego.   We ought not to speak of conscience before a super-ego is demonstrable ; as to consciousness of guilt, we must admit that it comes into being before the super-ego, therefore before conscience.   At that time it is the direct expression of the dread of external authority, the recognition of the tension between the ego and this latter ; it is the direct derivative of the conflict between the need for parental love and the urgency towards instinctual gratification, and it is the thwarting of this urgency that provokes the tendency to aggression. It is because these two different versions of the sense of guilt—one arising from dread of the external and the other from dread of the inner authority—are superimposed one on the other that our insight into the relations of conscience has been hampered in so many ways. Remorse is a general term denoting the ego's reaction under a special form of the sense of guilt; it includes the almost unaltered sensory material belonging to the anxiety that is at work behind the sense of guilt; it is itself a punishment and may include the need for punishment; it too, therefore, may occur before conscience has developed.

Further, it will do no harm for us to review once more the contradictions which have confused us at times during our enquiries. The sense of guilt, we said at one point, was the consequence of uncommitted aggressions; but another time and in particular in the case of its historical beginning, the murder of the father, it was the consequence of an aggression that was carried out. We also found a way out of this difficulty. The development of the inner authority, the super-ego, was precisely what radically altered the whole situation.   Before this, the sense of guilt coincided with remorse; we observe, in saying this, that the term remorse is to be reserved for the reaction after an actual performance of an aggressive deed.   After this, the omniscience of the super-ego robbed the distinction between intended aggressions and aggressions committed of its significance ; a mere intention to commit an act of violence could then evoke a sense of guilt—as psycho-analysis has found—as well as one which has actually been committed—as all the world knows.   The conflict of ambivalence between the two primal instincts leaves the same impress on the psychological situation, irrespective of the change that has taken place in this.   A temptation arises to look here for an explanation of the mystery of the varying relation between the sense of guilt and consciousness.   The sense of guilt which is due to remorse for an evil deed must always have been conscious ; that due to a perception of an evil impulse could have remained unconscious.   But it cannot be as simple as that : the obsessional neurosis contradicts it emphatically.   The second contradiction was that the aggressive energy with which one imagined the super-ego to be endowed was, according to one view, merely a continuation of the punitive energy belonging to external authority, preserved within the mind ; whereas according to another view it consisted, on the contrary, of aggressive energy originating in the self, levelled against this inhibiting authority but not allowed to discharge itself in actions. The first view seemed to accord better with the history of the sense of guilt, the second with the theory of it. More searching reflection has resolved this apparently irreconcilable contradiction almost too completely ; what remained as essential and common to both was that in both cases we were dealing with an aggression that had been turned inward. Clinical observation, moreover, really permits us to distinguish two sources for the aggressiveness we ascribe to the super-ego, each of which in any given case may be operating predominantly, but which usually are both at work together.

This, I think, is the place to suggest that a proposal which I previously put forward as a provisional assumption should be taken in earnest. In the latest analytical literature [1] a predilection has been shown for the view that any kind of privation, any thwarted instinctual gratification, results in a heightening of the sense of guilt, or

[1] In particular, in contributions by Ernest Jones, Susan Isaacs, Melanie Klein ; also, as I understand, in those of Reik and Alexander.

may do so.   I believe one obtains a great simplification of theory if one regards this as valid *only* for
the aggressive instincts, and that little will be
found to contradict this assumption.   How then
is it to be explained dynamically and economically
that a heightening of the sense of guilt should
appear in place of an unfulfilled erotic desire ?
This can surely only happen in a roundabout way :
the thwarting of the erotic gratification provokes
an access of aggressiveness against the person who
interfered with the gratification, and then this
tendency to aggression in its turn has itself to be
suppressed.   So then it is, after all, only the aggression which is changed into guilt, by being
suppressed and made over to the super-ego.   I am
convinced that very many processes will admit of
much simpler and clearer explanation if we re-
strict the findings of psycho-analysis in respect of
the origin of the sense of guilt to the aggressive
instincts.   Reference to the clinical material here
gives us no unequivocal answer, because, according
to our own hypothesis, the two kinds of instincts
hardly ever appear in a pure form, unmixed with
each other ; but the investigation of extreme cases
would probably point in the direction I anticipate.
I am tempted to extract our first advantage from
this narrower conception by applying it to the

repression-process.   The symptoms of neurosis, as we have learnt, are essentially substitutive gratifications for unfulfilled sexual wishes.   In the course of our analytic work we have found to our surprise that perhaps every neurosis masks a certain amount of unconscious sense of guilt, which in its turn reinforces the symptoms by exploiting them as punishment.   One is now inclined to suggest the following statement as a possible formulation : when an instinctual trend undergoes repression, its libidinal elements are transformed into symptoms and its aggressive components into a sense of guilt.   Even if this statement is only accurate as an approximation it merits our interest.

Some readers of this essay, too, may be under the impression that the formula of the struggle between Eros and the death instinct has been re-iterated too often.   It is supposed to characterize the cultural process which evolves in humanity ; but it has been related also to the development of the individual, and besides this, is supposed to have revealed the secret of organic life in general.   It becomes necessary for us to examine the relation of these three processes to one another.   Now, the repetition of the same formula is vindicated by the consideration that the cultural processes both in humanity and in the development of an individual are life-processes ; consequently they must both partake of the most universal characteristic of life. On the other hand, evidence of the presence of this universal characteristic does not help us to discriminate, unless it is further narrowed down by special qualifications. We can therefore set our minds at rest only if we say that the cultural process is the particular modification undergone by the life-process under the influence of the task set before it by Eros and stimulated by Ananke, external necessity ; and this task is that of uniting single human beings into a larger unity with libidinal attachments between them. When, however, we compare the cultural process in humanity with the process of development or upbringing in an individual human being, we shall conclude without much hesitation that the two are very similar in nature, if not in fact the same process applied to a different kind of object. The civilizing process in the human species is naturally more of an abstraction than the development of an individual, and therefore harder to apprehend in concrete terms, nor should the discovery of analogies be pushed to extremes ; but in view of the similar character of the aims of the two processes—in one the incorporation of an individual as a member of a group and in the other the creation

of a single group out of many individuals—the
similarity of the means employed and of the results
obtained in the two cases is not surprising. In
view of its exceptional importance, we must no
longer postpone mention of one feature differentiat-
ing the two processes. The development of the
individual is ordered according to the programme
laid down by the pleasure-principle, namely, the
attainment of happiness, and to this main objective
it holds firmly ; the incorporation of the individual
as a member of a community, or his adaptation
to it, seems like an almost unavoidable condition
which has to be filled before he can attain this
objective of happiness. If he could achieve it
without fulfilling this condition it would perhaps
be better. To express it differently, we may say :
individual development seems to us a product of
the interplay of two trends, the striving for happiness, generally called ' egoistic ', and the impulse
towards merging with others in the community,
which we call ' altruistic '. Neither of these de-
scriptions goes far beneath the surface. In individual development, as we have said, the main
accent falls on the egoistic trend, the striving for
happiness ; while the other tendency, which may
be called the ' cultural ' one, usually contents itself
with instituting restrictions. But things are differ-

ent in the development of culture : here far the most important aim is that of creating a single unity out of individual men and women, while the objective of happiness, though still present, is pushed into the background ; it almost seems as if humanity could be most successfully united into one great whole if there were no need to trouble about the happiness of individuals. The process of development in individuals must therefore be admitted to have its special features which are not repeated in the cultural evolution of humanity ; the two processes only necessarily coincide in so far as the first also includes the aim of incorporation into the community.

Just as a planet circles round its central body while at the same time rotating on its own axis, so the individual man takes his part in the course of humanity's development as he goes on his way through life. But to our dull eyes the play of forces in the heavens seems set fast in a never-varying scheme, though in organic life we can still see how the forces contend with one another and the results of the conflict change from day to day. So in every individual the two trends, one towards personal happiness and the other towards unity with the rest of humanity, must contend with each other ; so must the two processes of individual and of cultural development oppose each other and dispute the ground against each other. This struggle between individual and society, however, is not derived from the antagonism of the primal instincts, Eros and Death, which are probably irreconcilable ; it is a dissension in the camp of the libido itself, comparable to the contest between the ego and its objects for a share of the libido ; and it does eventually admit of a solution in the individual, as we may hope it will also do in the future of civilization—however greatly it may oppress the lives of individuals at the present time.

The analogy between the process of cultural evolution and the path of individual development may be carried further in an important respect. It can be maintained that the community, too, develops a super-ego, under whose influence cultural evolution proceeds. It would be an enticing task for an authority on human systems of culture to work out this analogy in specific cases. I will confine myself to pointing out certain striking details. The super-ego of any given epoch of civilization originates in the same way as that of an individual ; it is based on the impression left behind them by great leading personalities, men of outstanding force of mind, or men in whom some one human tendency has developed in unusual strength and purity, often for that reason very disproportionately. In many instances the analogy goes still further, in that during their lives—often enough, even if not always—such persons are ridiculed by others, ill-used or even cruelly done to death, just as happened with the primal father who also rose again to become a deity long after his death by violence. The most striking example of this double fate is the figure of Jesus Christ, if indeed it does not itself belong to the realm of mythology which called it into being out of a dim memory of that primordial event. Another point of agreement is that the cultural super-ego, just like that of an individual, sets up high ideals and standards, and that failure to fulfil them is punished by both with ' anxiety of conscience '. In this particular, indeed, we come across the remarkable circumstance that the mental processes concerned here are actually more familiar to us and more accessible to consciousness when they proceed from the group than they can be in the individual. In the latter, when tension arises, the aggressions of the super-ego voicing its noisy reproaches are all that is perceived, while its injunctions themselves often remain unconscious in the background. If we bring them to the knowledge of consciousness we find that they coincide with the demands of the prevailing cultural super-ego. At this point the two processes, that of the evolution of the group and the development of the indivudual, are always firmly mortised together, so to speak. Consequently many of the effects and properties of the super-ego can be more easily detected through its operations in the group than in the individual.

The cultural super-ego has elaborated its ideals and erected its standards. Those of its demands which deal with the relations of human beings to one another are comprised under the name of ethics. The greatest value has at all times been set upon systems of ethics, as if men had expected them in particular to achieve something especially important. And ethics does in fact deal predominantly with the point which is easily seen to be the sorest of all in any scheme of civilization. Ethics must be regarded therefore as a therapeutic effort : as an endeavour to achieve something through the standards imposed by the superego which had not been attained by the work of civilization in other ways. We already know—it is what we have been discussing—that the question is how to dislodge the greatest obstacle to civilization, the constitutional tendency in men to aggressions against one another ; and for that very reason the commandment to love one's neighbour as oneself—probably the most recent of the cultural super-ego's demands—is especially interesting to us.   In our investigations and our therapy of the neuroses we cannot avoid finding fault with the super-ego of the individual on two counts : in commanding and prohibiting with such severity it troubles too little about the happiness of the ego, and it fails to take into account sufficiently the difficulties in the way of obeying it—the strength of instinctual cravings in the id and the hardships of external environment.   Consequently in our therapy we often find ourselves obliged to do battle with the super-ego and work to moderate its demands.   Exactly the same objections can be made against the ethical standards of the cultural super-ego.   It, too, does not trouble enough about the mental constitution of human beings ; it enjoins a command and never asks whether or not it is possible for them to obey it.   It presumes, on the contrary, that a man's ego is psychologically capable of anything that is required of it—that his ego has unlimited power over his id.   This is an error ; even in so-called normal people the power of controlling the id cannot be increased beyond certain limits.   If one asks more of them, one produces revolt or neurosis in individuals or makes them unhappy.   The command to love our neighbours as ourselves is the strongest defence there is against human aggressiveness and it is a superlative example of the unpsychological attitude of the cultural super-ego. The command is impossible to fulfil ; such an enormous inflation of love can only lower its value and not remedy the evil. Civilization pays no heed to all this ; it merely prates that the harder it is to obey the more laudable the obedience. The fact remains that anyone who follows such preaching in the present state of civilization only puts himself at a disadvantage beside all those who set it at naught. What an overwhelming obstacle to civilization aggression must be if the defence against it can cause as much misery as aggression itself ! ' Natural ' ethics, as it is called, has nothing to offer here beyond the narcissistic satisfaction of thinking oneself better than others. The variety of ethics that links itself with religion brings in at this point its promises of a better future life. I should imagine that as long as virtue is not rewarded in this life ethics will preach in vain. I too think it unquestionable that an actual change in men's attitude to property would be of more help in this direction than any ethical commands ; but among the Socialists this proposal is obscured by new idealistic expectations disregarding human nature, which detract from its value in actual practice.

It seems to me that the point of view which seeks to follow the phenomena of cultural evolution as manifestations of a super-ego promises to yield still further discoveries. I am coming quickly to an end. There is one question, however, which I can hardly ignore. If the evolution of civilization has such a far-reaching similarity with the development of an individual, and if the same methods are employed in both, would not the diagnosis be justified that many systems of civilization—or epochs of it—possibly even the whole of humanity—have become ' neurotic ' under the pressure of the civilizing trends ? To analytic dissection of these neuroses therapeutic recommendations might follow which could claim a great practical interest. I would not say that such an attempt to apply psycho-analysis to civilized society would be fanciful or doomed to fruitlessness. But it behoves us to be very careful, not to forget that after all we are dealing only with analogies, and that it is dangerous, not only with men but also with concepts, to drag them out of the region where they originated and have matured. The diagnosis of collective neuroses, moreover, will be confronted by a special difficulty. In the neurosis of an individual we can use as a starting-point the contrast presented to us between the patient and his environment which we assume to be ' normal '. No such background as this would be available for any society similarly affected ; it would have to be supplied in some other way. And with regard to any therapeutic application of our knowledge, what would be the use of the most acute analysis of social neuroses, since no one possesses power to compel the community to adopt the therapy ? In spite of all these difficulties, we may expect that one day someone will venture upon this research into the pathology of civilized communities.

For various reasons, it is very far from my intention to express any opinion concerning the value of human civilization. I have endeavoured to guard myself against the enthusiastic partiality which believes our civilization to be the most precious thing that we possess or could acquire, and thinks it must inevitably lead us to undreamt-of heights of perfection. I can at any rate listen without taking umbrage to those critics who aver that when one surveys the aims of civilization and the means it employs, one is bound to conclude that the whole thing is not worth the effort and that in the end it can only produce a state of things which no individual will be able to bear. My impartiality is all the easier to me since I know very little about these things and am sure only of one thing, that the judgements of value made by mankind are immediately determined by their desires for happiness: in other words, that those judgements are attempts to prop up their illusions with arguments. I could understand it very well if anyone were to point to the inevitable nature of the process of cultural development and say, for instance, that the tendency to institute restrictions upon sexual life or to carry humanitarian ideals into effect at the cost of natural selection are developmental trends which it is impossible to avert or divert, and to which it is best for us to submit as though they were natural necessities. I know, too, the objection that can be raised against this: that tendencies such as these, which are believed to have insuperable power behind them, have often in the history of man been thrown aside and replaced by others. My courage fails me, therefore, at the thought of rising up as a prophet before my fellow-men, and I bow to their reproach that I have no consolation to offer them; for at bottom this is what they all demand—the frenzied revolutionary as passionately as the most pious believer.

The fateful question of the human species seems

to me to be whether and to what extent the cultural process developed in it will succeed in mastering the derangements of communal life caused by the human instinct of aggression and self-destruction. In this connection, perhaps the phase through which we are at this moment passing deserves special interest. Men have brought their powers of subduing the forces of nature to such a pitch that by using them they could now very easily exterminate one another to the last man. They know this—hence arises a great part of their current unrest, their dejection, their mood of apprehension. And now it may be expected that the other of the two ' heavenly forces ', eternal Eros, will put forth his strength so as to maintain himself alongside of his equally immortal adversary.

9 781891 396250